www.katsinsight.com

© 2016 Katrina Read

www.katsinsight.com

All rights reserved. No portion of this book may be reproduced in any form or by any means, electronic or mechanical, including photocopying, recording or by any information retrieval, without prior permission in writing from the publisher.

Any views and opinions expressed herein are strictly the author's own and do not represent those of any organisation.

DISCLAIMER

The content of this book is to serve as a general overview of matters of interest and is not intended to be comprehensive, nor does it constitute advice in any way. This book is a compilation of one person's ideas, concepts, ideologies, philosophies and opinions. You should carry out your own research and/or seek your own professional advice before acting or relying on any of the information displayed in this book. The author will not be liable for any loss or damage (financial or otherwise) that may arise out of your improper use of, or reliance on, the content of this book. You accept sole responsibility of the outcomes if you choose to adopt and/or use the ideas, concepts, ideologies, philosophies and opinions within the content of this book.

www.katsinsight.com

katbytes

One woman's love affair with data and analytics.

by **Katrina Read**

Dedicated to the clients that have challenged and inspired me, and the colleagues who have shared our journey.

www.katsinsight.com

www.katsinsight.com

Preface

A wise man once told me, some days you just have to **feed the family**, other days you'll get to **live the dream**. Since then, it's been a motto both in my personal life, and in my professional career.

In the world of big data and analytics, feeding the family means making sure data is managed, secured, cleansed, available, scalable, analysed and presented in a way that communicates insight and supports critical business decisions. Living the dream? Well that's those rare projects where we get to use data and insight to help make the world a better place!

This book captures some of my favourite articles that I've written over the past five years at **katsinsight.com** on my journey to helping clients find value in data. They include research on trends in the industry, useful tips and techniques, and great stories from clients I've had the pleasure of working with.

Together we've fed the family, lived the dream, and everything else in between.

xoxo

Kat

www.katsinsight.com

Table of Contents

Preface 5

Table of Contents 7

Feed The Family 9
    Marketing in the era of Cognitive 12
    ING Direct takes customer centricity to heart 21
    Geek Chic at Melbourne Spring Fashion Week 27
    Serving up a superior experience at the Australian Open 28
    WHAT IF? Advanced forecasting with Enterprise Planning and
    Predictive Analytics 33
    Planning, Budgeting and Forecasting Dinosnores 36
    Enterprise Planning: Linfox are in it for the long haul 40
    Delivering actionable insights at Citigroup 45
    From Rio to Roskilde: The real-life experiment for big data and
    sustainable cities 53
    Why information about assets is your greatest asset 56

Before You Start 59
    Generation D: Data-rich and analytically driven 61
    The Chief Data Officer (CDO): Tomorrow's corporate rockstar 64
    Big data? Big deal. 67
    5 Big Data Resolutions for the New Year 70
    The journey to Cognitive 76
    10 Reasons to get SaaS-y 83
    Business Analytics: Design Outcomes, Not Solutions 91
    The Yin Yang of BI 94
    Tackling the Tender: The 5 questions you need to ask 96

A Word About Customers 99
    The Connected Consumer is King 101
    What Mobile & Analytics have in common: The Consumer 104
    3 Caveats to Calling the Right Customer 110

| You have 30 seconds to make the right decision. Your time starts...NOW! | 114 |

Live The Dream 117
    Big Data. Big Cats. Big Hearts. 119
    Fighting Skin Cancer with Visual Analytics 121
    Race Across America with Analytics 123
    That's NEET! How Medway Youth Trust & SPSS are changing lives.... 128

About the author 131

Feed The Family

"Without data, you're just another person with an opinion."

W. Edwards Deming

www.katsinsight.com

www.katsinsight.com

Feeding the family is about making sure you are doing what it takes to survive (in the world of business) – when it comes to data and insight, there are a number of key business imperatives common to every organisation, across every industry.

First and foremost, the need to acquire, grow and retain customers, employees or citizens. This requires targeted acquisition, personalised marketing, and improved retention, with a strategic view of profitability.

The need to optimise operations, counter fraud and threats – through more intelligent business process operations, infrastructure and asset efficiency, factoring in public safety, security and defence.

The need to maximise insight, ensure trust and improve IT economics, by harnessing and analysing all available data, enabling a full spectrum of analytics, governing and protecting data, and optimising big data and analytics infrastructure.

And the need to transform financial and management processes, with improved planning and performance management, financial disclosures and managed risks.

The following are a selection of disruptive trends and case studies of organisations that are leading the way.

Marketing in the era of Cognitive

People talk about digital disruption as if it's the biggest challenge facing businesses today. Examples are plentiful - you only have to ask the taxi or hotel industry how much their business has been turned inside-out by the digital innovations brought to the table by Uber and Airbnb.

But is it really the use of digital leading the disruption?

This year I attended in the World Business Forum in Sydney, in which the co-founder of the MIT Media Labs discussed a number of key inventions from the 50s and 60s, including an Uber-type model. They created a computer program that could geo-locate people, and send cars to pick them up based on an optimisation algorithm. So what's different now? Why has it taken 50 years to be commercialised and become mainstream? No doubt the pervasive use of smartphones and digital technology played a significant role, but I propose the greatest disruption facing your business is you!

You, me, and the community of customers, consumers, colleagues and citizens around us. Why? Because with the simple flick of a finger we can SWIPE LEFT!!!

In the world of dating, we have the ability to swipe left. We can reject potential suitors before they even get a chance to deliver their best sales pitch - based purely on the way they are perceived in that first impression. We can swipe left on a bad hairstyle, on a questionable outfit, on the angle the photo has been taken.

www.katsinsight.com

But did you know your customers can swipe left on your marketing offers a well? Mobile devices allow you to view your inbox with a preview sentence - without even opening an email, a customer can decide whether your mail is worthy of opening for a closer look, or simply swipe left to send it to the trash. In a time when most companies still rely heavily on email marketing campaigns, how does it feel to know your latest catchy campaign may never see the light of day, simply because the customer has the power to swipe left?

Boring subject? Swipe left!

Generic greeting? Swipe left!

Wrong time of day? Swipe left!

In a world where people are time-poor and technology-rich, how do you capture the attention of a moving market?

You've no doubt heard the saying that a customer's last best experience is the minimum expectation they will have for every company and every interaction moving forward. But have you stopped to think about what that really means? It means the benchmark is always being raised. It's not just your competitors you have to worry about - it's every company, small and large, that interacts with your customers.

That amazing bank that makes mobile transactions super easy, is raising the bar on you.

That favourite retailer that sends personalised offers when the customer walks past their store, is raising the bar on you.

www.katsinsight.com

That innovative telco that put a personal support agent in your customer's pocket, 24x7, is raising the bar on you.

In a world awash with data, both structured and unstructured, growing at unprecedented rates, customers still expect you to hear them, make sense of it, and pre-empt their needs. Why? Because that bank, retailer or telco is doing it already! More than ever, customers are sharing information about their lives - their hopes, their dreams, their challenges. They expect you to listen, learn, and predict life events; fight to stop them from churning; understand and know their value; market products to them they are interested in; get the timing right; and design future products and services based on their feedback. They want you to be invested in them, as much as they are invested in you.

The Chief Design Officer at PepsiCo sums in up perfectly – *"Brands are no longer what we say about ourselves, but what our customers say about us."* And when customers are talking, they expect you to listen.

I'm not just referring to marketing being personalised. This is about marketing being person<u>al</u>. It's about communicating in a way that an individual customer appreciates and values. Personalisation is a top down approach - here's a set of campaigns, lets target customers based on these demographics or behaviours. Whereas being personal is a bottom up approach - here's a specific customer we value and an opportunity to market to them, let's create a message that will resonate. And it's not just about an offer or an action, but the value proposition and the language you use to deliver it.

> "Brands are no longer what we say about ourselves, but what our customers say about us."

Mauro Porcini, Chief Design Officer, PepsiCo

I believe there is a new battleground emerging around the future of customer experience, and it's centred around how you make your customers feel, think and act. Emotion is fast becoming the future of customer experience. They may not remember what you showed them or offered them, but they will remember how you made them feel. This is not simply customer satisfaction - satisfaction determines whether the customer will return a product or ask for a refund. No, this is much more than that! This is about whether the customer felt *excited, passionate, enlightened, amused, entertained, adored, respected, amazed*....enough to promote your brand to their friends and families with so much passion that their connections can't help but be caught up in the experience too.

Emotion is the future of customer experience, and cognitive computing is an enabler to understanding and influencing emotion.

Take for example Westfield San Francisco, who wanted to change the experience of buying someone a present from a stressful one, to a fun and enjoyable one. Imagine you are walking into a shopping centre, tasked with buying the perfect gift for a friend - only you have no idea what to buy! As a parent - I find myself in this situation almost on a weekly basis. So here you are, standing in the middle of a crowd, asking a series of questions - *how old are they? Boy or girl? Do they like sports? Do they like music?* How can I possibly choose something they'll love? Most of us probably just give up and aim for something they don't already have and/or won't mind getting - that's setting the bar pretty low and reducing the overall experience for the gift giver.

To flip the experience from a stressful one to an exciting adventure, Westfield San Francisco introduced the Westfield Virtual Personal

Shopper to match people to the brands and products they are most likely to love based on their personality. *Are they outgoing or reserved? Are they sensitive or confident?* By providing an individual's social profile, we are able to analyse the language and sentiment used to determine an individual's personality traits, and match them to brands and products that resonate with that particular personality profile. Let's consider the same demographic - same age, gender and location, but different personality profiles. One individual is self-expressive, and loves a challenge - the Virtual Personal Shopper might recommend a new set of kicks. But for someone who shows strong practical and conservative traits, it might recommend a good quality wallet. With the gift of insight, shopping for a birthday present becomes fun, exciting, and even intriguing.

Imagine walking into a department store and being greeted by an adorable robot: *"Hiya Kat!"* (That's how I like to be greeted by the way.) *"Great to see you in store. I found the perfect pair of shoes to match that bag you bought last week - would you like me to take you to it?"* Sound futuristic? It's not - retailers around the world are bringing the power of cognitive computing into the store to make it personal. It doesn't feel like an up-sell/cross-sell campaign, it doesn't feel like a marketing ad, it feels personal - this store knows me, what I love, and what I can't say *"no"* to.

Cognitive computing doesn't just understand and learn natural language, it also analyses images and videos too. Once you know a customer's personality, you can also pick the perfect image to include in that targeted offer - one that is going to invoke the right emotion that gets them to click, to buy, to act!

www.katsinsight.com

Of course, if you're going to make it personal, it has to be on the customer's terms, at a time that is convenient to them. Customers shouldn't have to work around our opening times or preferred channels. When my husband is eating breakfast at 7am and checks his sports twitter feed - that's when you target him on the iPad. After the kids are in bed, and I'm sitting down at 8:30pm to catch up on TV, that's when you target me on my mobile. And at either of those times, day and night, someone needs to be there to answer our questions and help us take action - except maybe that someone isn't necessarily human, but a computer trained to think like a human that can guide the customer through the decision process.

In the era of Cognitive, marketing becomes less about selling, and more about educating, engaging and advising.

It's more than just being able to serve up the right offer at the right time, it's about being able to follow through to purchase. How frustrating is it to execute a fantastic marketing campaign, only to have customers drop out of the purchase process when they can't find the product or service they need? Using cognitive computing, companies are creating personal shopping assistants and online agents to make sure customers get the help they need to close on a purchase each and every time, day or night.

Take The North Face for example, when directed to their website, customers can engage with the personal shopping assistant to help them find the right product by answering a series of questions about where they are travelling to. Combining product information, with climate data, the personal shopping assistant can make recommendations and revise as the customer shares more about what they are looking for - colour, size, style etc. The customer doesn't need to know that behind the scenes their personal shopping assistant is actually a computer, consuming information from product and geography websites to understand the specific needs of the customer, make recommendations, and converse using natural language.

Similarly, Wayblazer uses cognitive computing to provide a personal travel assistant to each and every customer - helping them along their purchasing journey. Based on the questions and answers from the customer, their website learns the types of activities a customer is interested in, and makes recommendations on what events they would most love. Again, no need for the customer to know the person helping them make their trip the best experience possible, is actually a computer.

Cognitive computing will no doubt change the game in how we connect and engage with our customers, but it's also going to fundamentally revolutionise the way marketing professionals connect and engage with technology too. Cognitive commerce is fast becoming the future of work.

Marketing professionals will be able to leverage the power of cognitive to understand which text, images and videos are having the best impact, and which are best suited to the personality of their target audience. A platform in which you can evaluate the performance of individual campaign assets, and tweak them accordingly to get a better response. A tool in which you can view a single view of a product or brand - including both an internal perspective, and external sentiment from social media and news sources. The ability to conduct market research across both structured and unstructured data in one instance. But most

"In the era of Cognitive, marketing becomes less about selling, and more about educating, engaging and advising."

www.katsinsight.com

importantly, a platform that speaks your language - in which you can engage in a dialogue to navigate, question, discover and refine marketing campaigns for maximum efficiency. An era in which your marketing tools speak your language, not the other way around.

Today, customer expectation of the companies that serve them is based on their last best experience. But tomorrow, the expectation will be "*If computers can understand me, why can't you?*". The question you have to ask yourself, as marketing moves into the era of cognitive computing, will you, or your competitors, be next to raise the bar?

ING Direct takes customer centricity to heart

I had the privilege of listening to Glen Comerford, the Marketing Analytics Manager for ING Direct, talk about their exciting journey to becoming one of the most customer-centric banks in Australia.

Glen speaks passionately about the conflict between putting customers first versus a commercial outcome, and the fact that nine times out of ten, commercial outcomes will win on priority and the customer will take second place. Take for example Ikea, where stores are designed more like mazes, intent on keeping customers in the store as long as possible to maximise the basket size. But in doing so, many customers come out of the store purchasing things they didn't need (and later regret), and make note to avoid all future visits unless it's absolutely necessary. This ultimately leaves a negative customer experience and lower chance of return visits - some might argue it even reduces the overall lifetime value of each customer. Milk at the supermarket is another classic example - always located at the back of the store in the hopes that you'll pick up a few other items on your way down the aisle - items you probably didn't need. As a result, anyone that just wants a litre of milk, is probably going to avoid a supermarket at all costs!

Glen's premise however, is that we need to switch the lens from how big we can make a customer's basket spend, to how much we can get from a customer throughout their life - an increased focus on lifetime value which fundamentally requires companies to put customer centricity at the heart of every business initiative.

With an NPS score of +28, compared to -6 for most Australian banks, it stands to reason that ING Direct are the experts in customer centricity - providing 2% cash back at the register when paying with an ING card, $0 monthly fees, low interest rates, and free use of any ATM (yes, ANY ATM!!!), they certainly have the products and services to back it up.

But that wasn't always the case.

Back in 2014, Glen reflects that ING communications were prioritised based on business needs. When a new insurance product was released - the goal was to sell it to all their customers. Measurement of performance was based on direct measures, such as the number of clicks, opens and unsubscribes - none of which actually measure ultimate success for ING or value for their clients. As a result of marketing being incentivised on clicks and opens, targeting of campaigns was isolated to those customer groups with the proven highest level of direct response - not customers who were most likely to buy.

Recognising the need to change, ING started out by asking two questions:

1. How do customers behave after we contact them? And more importantly;

2. How would they behave if we had done nothing? Unfortunately, very few companies ask this question.

What they found was that just 5% of direct marketing campaigns were delivering 90% of the results, 70% had no meaningful impact at all, and 10% had a material negative impact on customer behaviour. One such example was a campaign headline *"Get a bonus $300 free travel"*, but the terms and conditions were so onerous not many customers could actually fulfil them - as a result clients were left feeling at best disappointed, at worst ripped off, causing them to go elsewhere.

With a fresh perspective on the importance of customer centricity when making decisions about their marketing campaigns, immediate action was taken. Under-performing campaigns were shut down (80% of all campaigns), the highest performing historical campaigns were repeated and expanded (5%), and with freed up capacity, resources were reassigned to focus on innovation.

Putting the customer at the heart of business decisions delivered a sustained three times greater performance in cross-buy campaigns, which at one point delivered up to fifteen times greater results. Measurement was shifted from direct marketing response, to total customer behaviour.

A new challenge then arose - when you dramatically increase the success of marketing campaigns, more customers naturally have more products, and since there's only so many times you can buy the same product or service, continuous innovation became the key to maintaining ongoing success.

One of the main enablers of this evolution was the ability to move from a monologue type engagement to an ongoing dialogue. Instead of sending out a blanket email to all customers about a new mortgage product in the off chance they might want to sign up for it, they targeted specific customers when they logged onto the website - clicking on a banner registers interest in the system and triggers an outbound call within 24 hours. If the customer is ready to proceed - the sales process begins. If not, the system allows them to keep leads warm with relevant content via email and Facebook, scheduling calls back when the customer is ready to purchase.

In 2015, Glen reflects they faced a similar re-targeting challenge in the digital space as faced in marketing. With digital advertising, a customer registering interest in a product or service is suddenly targeted with offers on all devices, even after they've made a purchase. At best this can be creepy or annoying, at worst, they may even see a better offer and be left angry that they accepted a substandard offer. ING wanted to serve content to people based on total behaviour, across all devices, making sure if a customer already owns products, they are not targeted with the same products again.

The business case to invest in technology to make this happen was clear in Glen's mind - more relevant advertising, better use of resources, improved measurement, and anticipated three times performance gains on digital media.

Today, ING can target people online through digital media with the same precision you could offline through email campaigns and direct mail. A unique customer ID is created in the digital world to connect to various ad-buying platforms with control groups, and a greater understanding of online and offline behaviour.

Based on the journey that Glen and ING Direct Australia embarked on, he has three recommendations for companies wishing to put customers at the heart of business decisions:

1. Find out what customers did after you contacted them, and what they could have done if you hadn't contacted them at all.

2. Quantify the proportion of your marketing activity that adds no value, and eliminate it.

3. The age of click-based attribution and investment is coming to an end - get ready with a solution that puts the customer at the centre of your digital media.

"Technology has become the fabric in which brands and retailers can connect with consumers to understand them better and give them what they want."

Geek Chic at Melbourne Spring Fashion Week

Having worked in a male-dominated industry my entire career, surrounded by people with a love of all things technology, it was a breath of fresh Melbourne spring air when IBM was named the innovation and technology partner for Melbourne Spring Fashion Week (MSFW).

Historically, technology geeks and fashionistas lived in very different social circles. So what does technology and fashion have in common that now finds them joined at the hip? YOU!

We are part of a culture that embeds Social, Mobile and Location based technology (often referred to as "SoLoMo") into the very fabric of our lives.

We are influenced by what our friends and family have to say about services and products, and we aren't afraid to share our experiences through social media – both good and bad. In fact, 32% of us have shared a retail experience on social media, making social media analytics an essential tool for retailers to understand market sentiment and take the necessary actions to address issues in their business, and tap in to brand ambassadors to capitalise on positive sentiment.

We have increasing expectations of retailers – demanding a personalised experience whether we are in store, online, or using a mobile device. We want retailers to know who we are, what we like, and only to interact with us when it suits us.

www.katsinsight.com

Many retailers are still afraid to overstep the boundaries of consumer privacy, and yet 34% of us are willing to share current location information with our favourite retailers – and we expect them to do something with it! Whether it's offering a discount for dropping by the store, or helping us find products in store that we've been perusing in the online catalogue.

And if you thought it was just Millennials driving this change, think again. The average age of the SoLoMo trailblazer is 42 years old!

IBM partnered with the City of Melbourne to immerse consumers in the celebration of Australian fashion, providing access to information about events and brands through mobile devices, insight into behaviour and sentiment of MSFW guests through social media and data analytics, all hosted via an elastic cloud infrastructure to ensure insight can still be delivered during times of peak demand.

Technology and fashion are more than just joined at the hip. Technology has become the fabric in which brands and retailers can connect with consumers to understand them better and give them what they want.

Serving up a superior experience at the Australian Open

Time to slip on a shirt, slop on the sunscreen, slap on a hat, and head down to Melbourne's spectacular sporting precinct to revel in the summer excitement unique to the Australian Open.

Every year, Tennis Australia produces innovative ways to engage audiences both at the event, and around the world – bringing the fans closer to the thrill of the game, the players and the community spirit. With eight years of Grand Slam data providing players the ability to fine-tune their game, giving fans insight into how their favourite player is progressing against key performance indicators, and monitoring how public sentiment changes throughout the game and the event.

In addition to the eight years of Grand Slam data analysed, they also collect real-time data from umpires, statisticians, social media, and crowd mobile devices. This information is broadcast in real-time to a broad audience including the media, broadcasters, the all-important serve speed clock, scoreboards, player summary scorecards, information towers on site, smartphones and the official Australian Open website, just to name a few! This critical information is not just to engage fans, but also to ensure smooth operations over the two-week period to deliver a superior experience to attendees, players and support staff.

Here's some of my favourite examples of how analytics is used to engage players, fans and broadcasters at the Australian Open:

Slamtracker and Keys to the Match

One of my personal favourites, Slamtracker monitors each match in real time – such as serves, points, forced/unforced errors, momentum etc. – and identifies the three crucial actions each player can make on court that will have the biggest impact on their success. These "Keys to the Match" are based on insight derived from over 41 million data points of historical performance, coupled with the real-time statistics to identify the top critical success factors for a particular player, opponent and match conditions.

Slamtracker also includes player and ball tracking, including where the ball lands, along with how far a player runs in a given match. This adds a new dimension to match analysis, and will no doubt uncover new patterns and insights into player performance that could impact the outcome of a match. Keep your eye on Slamtracker during a match to watch how their on-court performance alters their chance of winning.

Social Sentiment

Slamtracker also analyses social media sentiment – monitoring whether people are saying positive or negative things about a specific player's on court and off court performance in real time. This helps Tennis Australia engage fans, as well as guide news stories and focus areas on the website and social media platforms.

Check out the Social Leaderboard on the Australian Open website to see who is being talked about most throughout the event! This is one page I know sponsors in particular will want to keep an eye on to see which players have the most positive influence with fans on social media.

CrowdTracker

Tennis Australia also uses live data collected through GPS tracking and Wi-Fi enabled devices to give fans at the event real-time insight into where they are on site to help them navigate around the precinct. This includes information about which matches are currently being played on which courts, coupled with interactive real-time scores for the match, player bios, social sentiment etc. It also shows them where the biggest crowds are so they can quickly head to the most popular spots (or avoid them if they prefer!), and popular Instagram spots and other social media activity so fans can get involved.

Operations Dashboard

Behind the scenes, analytics is used by Tennis Australian to manage the logistics of the event. The Operations Dashboard provides a deeper view of what's happening throughout the event, with real-time insight into areas such as merchandise, food and beverage, court services and tournament car usage. When a situation occurs that requires immediate intervention, the Tennis Australian crew are notified and provided with a recommended next best action.

What's really incredible, is that all this technology infrastructure is supported on the cloud. Resources are scaled up and down throughout the event to meet demand and ensure a positive user experience. Whilst the number of users has grown by 45% since 2008, the cost per user has decreased by 35%! Page views have increased by 42%, but cost per page view has decreased by 34%. A great example of how cloud technology makes innovation more cost-effective to businesses today.

Of course, this isn't just about applying cool technology to have some fun – there is serious value being generated here:

- Players and coaches have access to real-time match statistics and predictive insight to help them tweak their game plan, as well as critical information on the tournament and scheduling at their fingertips to take the stress out of the event and allow them to focus on doing what they do best – win!

- Broadcasters have access to real-time scoring and statistics feeds, game vision, graphics production, and tournament information and scheduling to ensure they can provide up-to-date information to their viewers that is interesting and keeps them engaged throughout the two-week event.

- Media has access to vision, graphics and social insight to create interesting stories around the event.

- Tennis fans have access to the information they need to maximise their personal experience – whether it's via a website from the comfort of their living room, or via a mobile device when they're at the event in person.

- Tennis Australia have the insight they need to execute a premier sporting event, ensuring a positive experience for all stakeholders.

This is undoubtedly one of my favourite times of the year – when great weather (most of the time) meets a great city. When great sport meets great technology. When work meets play.

WHAT IF? Advanced forecasting with Enterprise Planning and Predictive Analytics

WHAT IF?

Two of the most powerful words in the English language that confirm uncertainty and open the opportunity for understanding. In the world of business, how an organisation addresses these two simple words can determine those that succeed and those that struggle to compete.

WHAT IF you had an intimate understanding of the performance of your organisation?

WHAT IF you could evaluate the impact of your decisions on business outcomes?

The ability to understand the conditions in which you are operating and evaluate the impact of your decisions can give the competitive edge needed to survive in today's markets. Whether you are a retailer competing for market share, a government department providing much needed services to the community, a utility dealing with volatile resources, or a financial institution balancing profit with customer satisfaction.

In its simplest form, what-if analysis can be conducted using a Microsoft Excel spreadsheet with embedded rules and calculations, allowing you to adjust key factors and see how they impact the final outcome. Unfortunately, this approach is difficult to manage and secure, and is constrained to a single desktop. This minimises the ability for a team of experts, managers or executives to collaborate and provide input to the scenario analysis, resulting in spreadsheets being manually edited and emailed around teams. For these reasons, my customers often refer to it as "Excel Hell".

We can balance the ease of use in Microsoft Excel with an Enterprise Planning platform, delivering what-if analysis at the speed of thought. What this means to your business, is people across teams can collaborate on key factors that drive performance, and evaluate a range of business scenarios. Contributions are collected from team members and summarised at the corporate level – providing insight into performance throughout all levels of the organisation. A range of scenarios can be defined and evaluated until the decision makers are happy with the expected outcomes and can execute the best course of action.

WHAT IF you knew what was likely to happen minutes, hours, days, weeks, months from now? Would this change your decision?

Most organisations plan and evaluate forecasts based on historical performance and gut feel. A more powerful approach is to incorporate knowledge about what is likely to happen in the future, based on the hidden trends and patterns in the historical data that isn't necessarily obvious to the human eye. This "prediction" can become the baseline for the plan, with opportunity for decision makers to make adjustments and evaluate various scenarios based on both known- and previously unknown- relationships.

"WHAT IF you knew what was likely to happen minutes, hours, days, weeks, months from now?

Would this change your decision?"

By integrating Enterprise planning with predictive analytics, we can deliver advanced modelling and scenario analysis via a single, easy-to-use modelling worksheet for business users.

Customers around the world are getting smarter about how they evaluate their business scenarios. At the 2012 Business Analytics Forum, a much loved and widely respected Aussie brand, Australia Post, talked about this very topic – how they predict cash flow over a period, then adjust and evaluate scenarios to maximise the use of available resources, delivering significant benefit to the business.

WHAT IF you were the first in your market to leverage the power of Enterprise planning and predictive analytics for advanced forecasting and gained the competitive edge?

Planning, Budgeting and Forecasting Dinosnores

Every now and then you hear a story about a local organisation that leaves you thinking *"I never knew they did that!"* That was the case for me and a hundred of my closest friends at the 2016 Finance Forum, where Paul Ryan, the Chief Financial Officer of the Australian Museum, gave us insight into their business, their mission, and how they tackle the difficult challenge of planning, budgeting and forecasting for the age of dinosaurs and beyond.

The first myth Paul debunked, was that the Australian Museum is *just a building you can take your kids to to learn about history.* The mission of the Australian Museum is to be at the forefront of scientific research, collection and education, with the aim of procuring rare and curious specimens of natural history, and to inspire young people to take up science. With over 222 full time employees, 540 volunteers and a $772 Million business – it requires a little more than just selling a ticket at the door to keep it operating.

Fun fact: Did you know the Australian Museum has over 18 Million cultural and scientific objects, but just less than 1% on show at any point in time? Imagine the size of their closet!!!

You might think running a Museum is a simple business – not so. The two major parts of the business – Exhibitions and Science – are supported by an extensive set of business operations – from events, collections, heritage buildings, commercial venues and sponsorships, treasury and machinery of Government, grants, projects, and media delivered to the public via digital channels. Each requiring meticulous planning and budgeting to ensure smooth operations.

One of the critical functions of the Australian Museum is to attract and successfully display exhibitions – it's the lifeblood of their business, both bringing in revenue and maintaining relevance over their 188 years in operation. In addition to permanent and traveling gallery exhibitions owned by the Museum, they compete on an international stage to attract temporary exhibits such as the Aztecs and the Wildlife Photographer of the Year, with planning for each starting five years in advance. One of the key measurements of success by the Government is social relevance and ticket sales – so attracting the right exhibitions and maximising attendance is critical to their success and the success of attracting future exhibits.

www.katsinsight.com

The Australian Museum also has an international reputation for scientific research, cataloguing and describing over 100 new species in the last twelve months alone. Projects include habitat, impacts and migration studies on the pesky Indian Myna and Noise Miner, and how leaving corridors of trees (such as down the middle of a main road) is driving out local birds and supporting the growth of the pest. They provide scientific support to Australian and International authorities on the body parts trade of endangered species such as shark fin, rhino horns and ivory. They investigate aircraft bird strike, identifying bird species so they can study them and mitigate the risk of it happening again. They even operate a world-leading research station on Lizard Island with on-reef facilities for coral reef research and education – working tirelessly to find ways to save the future of the Great Barrier Reef.

With such an important focus on research, you can imagine how frustrating it would be to expect scientists to spend valuable time inputting timesheets or capturing data – that's time away from research and doing what they do best.

When Paul joined the Museum in 2014, on the last day of the financial year (!!!), he was faced with a number of challenges:

- Management reporting was all done in spreadsheets, with data downloaded from SAP and massaged into line items. There was no integrity in the numbers.

- There was virtually no forecasting at all – it was all focused on where the money was spent. Data often updated at the last minute – overnight the Museum went from a $1 Million surplus to a $40,000 deficit due to prepayments put into the system on June 30.

- There was no visibility into whether people were working on completing their budgets, which meant it would often be left to the last minute when reminders were communicated.

- Some people across the business were finding it difficult to use SAP, and needed a quicker and easier way to plan their budgets so they could focus on their jobs, not data entry.

Paul remembers his first board meeting well because the numbers didn't add up! People had forgotten to add activity from a new account in SAP into the spreadsheet – a mistake common in manually-created reports.

At the end of March 2015, the Australian Museum went live with Enterprise Planning to streamline their financial planning, budgeting and forecasting process. With a more user-friendly, Enterprise Planning platform, Paul was able to move to a bottom-up budgeting process, giving ownership to the 27 profit/cost centre managers and 20 grant/project managers instead of finance controlling the spreadsheets. So far the feedback from the business has been overwhelmingly positive, with people loving the new system due to its ease of use – they are now updating their forecasts directly into the planning system on a monthly basis.

The Australian Museum now has historical data available and reconciled, labour models created and integrated, assumptions behind the budget documented in detail, and a greater level of integrity in the numbers. Enterprise Planning gave the finance team more visibility into which cost centre managers had started preparing their budgets, and which needed a gentle nudge to get started. The team also has instant access to management reporting and the ability to drill down to investigate numbers – which means users can find answers themselves instead of kicking off email threads to validate and diagnose.

This year was the first time anyone had finished a budget before June 30 in the history of the museum. In fact, the first streamlined budget was completed before the end of May – less than two months after go live!

Moving forward, the Australian Museum is now looking at ways to incorporate predictive analytics for greater insight into admission analysis and better accuracy of forecasting models.

On a personal note, I'm always looking for new and exciting places to take my kids in the school holidays – I'm officially adding the Dinosnores sleepover program to our bucket list! And while the kids lie there in their sleeping bags thinking about the Zebras, Giraffes and Bears around them, I'll be appreciating all the work that's gone on behind the scenes to plan and prepare an opportunity to bring out the imagination of my budding little scientists.

Enterprise Planning: Linfox are in it for the long haul

In my first post for 2016, it was only natural I reflected on the wonderful few weeks I had spending time with family and friends, overindulging in too many delicious treats and beverages, and watching young and old enjoy quality time together - whether it's battling it out in a *very serious* game of backyard cricket, or teaching our youngest to ride a bike.

But while I sat there and enjoyed the festivities, I spared a thought for the people working tirelessly around the clock to make sure I had access to everything I needed to celebrate the perfect silly season - making sure the kids' Christmas presents were in store when I went to purchase them, to ensuring duck fat was in stock at my local supermarket shelves for the perfect roast potatoes.

One such team of secret Christmas Elves is Linfox, Australia's largest privately owned logistics company, with over 23,000 employees across 10 countries working to deliver adaptable supply chains for some of the world's largest retailers and consumer products companies. Managing 4.8 million square metres of warehouse and 5,000 individual trucks and equipment on road and rail across 250 separate operations, it's no small feat to deliver service excellence and real-time contact with operations around the clock.

Narayan Prasad, the Chief Financial Offer for Linfox Australia, gave insight at the Finance Forum 2016 into some of the work that goes on behind the scenes to ensure smooth operations with integrated planning across the business.

It was just a few years ago they faced a high level of dissatisfaction around planning and forecasting - providing the perfect catalyst for change. As an organisation, they faced a number of challenges:

- There was minimal linkage between strategy, long term plans and budgets.

- Planning was time consuming, with the budget process taking over six months to complete.

- There was a low level of credibility with no budget ownership and a manual-intensive process that was prone to errors.

- Plans were too detailed with a lack of focus on key drivers. For example, travel budget was derived based on the number of trips each person did, which created a vast amount of data that didn't actually improve the quality of the budget in any way.

- The process was inflexible - even small changes such as a salary increase required major rework and lengthy delays.

As a result, plans produced a high level of conservatism and were not accepted broadly by the board.

Narayan and his team introduced Enterprise Planning to re-focus their efforts across three key areas: People, Process and Systems.

They created a linkage between strategy, long terms plans and budgets. Instead of going straight to site budgets and making corporate cuts along the way, they incorporated strategic reviews prior to the start of the planning process so that long term financial goals would include value for shareholders and return on investment. This formed the framework for the following year's budget.

They simplified the design and stability of the process, focusing on key business drivers with incremental development of features to keep the platform relatively stable. Providing a consistent look and feel to the system also cut development time and gave greater stability, and delivered increased usability and relevance to the people that use it. They also made an important design decision to link the corporate planning solution to their ERP and other systems to provide consistent profit centres and account hierarchies with automated updates - they have not tried to recreate capabilities of other systems.

They put renewed focus on the ease of use for the contributors, with the important need to be usable by site managers in particular. To make it easier for site managers, centralised planning was done for some cost elements such as depreciation of existing assets, occupancy costs, work cover costs, insurance etc., automated calculations were incorporated for salary and wage costs, depreciation of new assets, and prior period data was made readily available. Users only had to input data related to revenue, wages, and discretionary costs. Working on remote sites, they also adapted the solution to meet the requirements of the users, with templates used to input budget data that had the look and feel of Excel spreadsheets, percolated with centrally planned data. With unreliable connectivity in some remote sites across Asia, it was critical site managers could input data offline and publish to the enterprise plan when they were back online.

Change management was also a major challenge due to the geographical spread of sites. Over 100 training sessions were conducted over two years - some face-to-face and others using web conferencing facilities. With a large number of users in non-English speaking environments, simplicity in systems and processes was essential.

With a renewed focus on ease of use and templates, system-generated forecasts as a starting point, availability of spreading tools to edit forecasts at a high level, and easy to use reports for all levels of management, Linfox created a more flexible planning process with greater user acceptance, increased credibility and most importantly, plans that were directly linked to the strategic goals of the business.

What does this mean for me? It means I can be certain that next Christmas I'll be able to indulge in far too many Tim Tams than necessary because they'll make sure those bit-sized chunks of heaven make it from source to store in time for my cuppa. Unfortunately, I made the mistake of showing my daughter, Jessica, Narayan's photo of the Giraffe they delivered to Perth Zoo - which by the way is her *favourite* animal. At least I know if she asks Santa for one next year, Linfox will be able to deliver!

Linfox have had a great motto in which they run their logistics business - but I think it can equally apply to their ability to plan and align their operations to their corporate strategy: "*Every site. Every day. Linfox leads the way.*"

Delivering actionable insights at Citigroup

This is a story about transformation. About radically changing the way an organisation thinks about data and self-service. About embarking on a journey to leverage data to achieve business goals – in this case, providing a better customer experience and managing expenses.

It's a story about Citigroup, one of the world's leading financial services company, providing consumers, corporations, governments and institutions with financial products and services around the world.

Laurie Kenski, Senior Vice President, Portfolio Manager at Citigroup, shared their story about driving change and reducing costs at Insight 2015.

Before their transformation journey began, Citigroup struggled to understand what fundamentally drives expenses, questioning whether they should even be in the business of certain products without truly knowing and understanding the driving forces behind the cost to serve. Their journey began in the employee help desk, with a view to provide the tools desperately need to run more efficient operations, provide decision support, and get closer to the voice of the customer.

"Help desks are tricky to optimise, and tricky to lean." explains Laurie. The main tool is human capital. At the core they are driven by people, which means driving change fundamentally impacts the

human condition. There is an ongoing struggle to find the sweet spot between customer experience and expense – and that's the exact challenge Citigroup decided to tackle head on.

The Citigroup call centre is no shrinking violet. With over 300,000 clients across 93 countries, supporting 20 languages and processing more than 100,000 tickets each and every month, agents across eight regional help desk locations work tirelessly to serve and support a growing global workforce.

Culturally, Citigroup employees had a low tolerance for the existing self-help solutions. With a propensity to throw work over the wall to level two support, more than 50% tickets opened were moved to higher cost service providers, even though 60% were not actually experiencing technology-related problems. They very much worked with a *"One Stop Shop"* mentality, depending heavily on someone else helping them find a solution.

This is what they wanted, *needed*, to change. Laurie describes it as giving them *"something intriguing to go to. We want them to think 'It's just like how I get help in my real life.' We're not shoving work on you, we're empowering you."*

In 2013, Citigroup began work to build out an analytical platform, bringing data in from key sources including ResolveIT, ServiceNow and Remedy, transforming it into useable form, augmenting with predictive and advanced insight and presenting key valuable insights to the business to help them make more effective decisions and drive change.

> "It's important to put it all together and tell stories about the data.
>
> Give them the context in which to make the decision."

Beth Rudden, Distinguished Engineer, IBM

www.katsinsight.com

Beth Rudden, an emerging technical leader and all-round analytical rock star, spearheaded the technical solution for the Citigroup call centre. She humorously compares the solution to a turbine engine – *"you suck things in, you compress, you ignite, then you blow it out."* Most organisations are getting pretty good at the *suck things in*, *compress*, and *blow it out* phases. But Beth really wanted to focus in on the ignition point – what's going to ignite the analytical engine that fundamentally transforms data to insight? In her view, it was the injection of predictive and advanced analytics that took Citigroup's data to the next level and ignited change within the business.

But that wasn't the only critical piece. She also stresses the importance of ensuring insights are visualised in a way that business users can consume and understand. Given that 90% of information comes into our brain through the visual vortex, as humans, we are created to find and recognise patterns. Close your eyes and imagine a million records in a database – there's no understanding in that. But imagine it on a map, and you can instantly recognise that one particular country has 20 tickets open and needs more focus. Within the analytic platform, they measured the past in order to predict the future, and used a range of visualisation techniques including geo-spatial, word clouds, correlation and causation charts. *"It's important to put it all together and tell stories about the data"*, Beth points out, *"to make people aware of what this means to them. Give them the context in which to make the decision."*

The inclusion of both structured and unstructured call data is also critical in understanding not just how the call centre works, but how business works, and what the customer really thinks.

They pulled together a team of specialists to design and build an underlying analytics platform that could ingest both structured and unstructured data, and deliver on the business objectives. From a technology perspective, Beth breaks the analytics platform down into four fundamental parts:

1. The hard part: This is the *"suck and muck"*. Combine, cleanse and match data from multiple structured and unstructured data sources.

2. The really hard part: Apply business rules to make sense of the data and add context, powered by predictive and advanced analytics, and data transformation tools.

3. The really really hard part: Re-frame the data as facts and dimensions in terms that make sense to the business so it can be more easily understood.

4. The sexy part: Visualise the abstractions to make sense for the customer. Give the end user the freedom to choose what works from them, and empower them to self-serve.

The Citigroup analytic platform ingests 292 million ServiceNow records, 310 million ResolveIT records, and consumes and processes data generated by over 120,000 real time calls daily.

When a call was answered, they didn't just solve the problem. They took the data and reapplied it to change the underlying root causes. They monitored everything over time – not just call completion times and categories, but also tapped into the unstructured data in the call records in order to aggregate all data, understand patterns and trends, decide a course of action, implement change and monitor over time.

And the results of the transformation are impressive.

Over time, fewer calls were coming into the call centre because they were fixing root causes.

Chuck Limoges, Senior Vice President of Infrastructure at Citigroup, stated that in the past nine months, they have reduced the time a ticket is open by a staggering 50%! Partly because half of all incidents providing educational or navigational assistance are now routed to employee self-service. Self-service that had been injected a new lease of life with fresh new content, IT expos, marketing brochures and campus educational campaigns. In parallel with the data transformation, a big focus was put on changing the culture so self-service becomes the norm.

A positive side effect from the transformational journey was that 1,800 primary applications were identified and removed as part of the initial data quality clean up – providing added benefits to expense management and IT complexity.

This particular phase of Citigroup's journey, started with the business, and ended with transformation. Laurie estimates they have saved millions of dollars in 2015 alone, with measurable reductions in duplicate and withdrawn tickets, and realised benefit in level two task elimination and shift left. With a drastically remodelled, re-branded self-help experience, Citigroup achieved both ticket reduction and a better client experience.

Of importance here is the fact that Citigroup never made it about metrics to measure productivity. What they were able to achieve wasn't just insight, but an empowered workforce and optimised price per cost to serve that fundamentally changes the way the business operates moving forward.

When asked what advice she would give to other customers looking to embark on a data transformation journey, Beth advises:

1. Day-to-day operations start with data. It starts with business, and it ends with insight. Make it as accessible as possible to as many people as possible – democratisation of analytics is key. Shift left!

2. Long term, remember that big change happens with many small instrumental changes. Small steps can have a bigger impact than people realise.

3. Trust is the right type of partnership. Beth attributes their success to the strength of the project team as they *"were able to understand the business – then render all measurements against business goals so customers have context as to what they are seeing."*

Chuck attributes their results to building for long term success. Focus on creating the right customer experience, achieve target cost outcomes, and reshape the workplace to create the right culture and engagement. *"We've made it our business, to use data to run our business. Our story could be your story."*

> "We've made it our business, to use data to run our business. Our story could be your story."

Chuck Limoges, Senior Vice President of Infrastructure, Citigroup

From Rio to Roskilde: The real-life experiment for big data and sustainable cities

In 2015, I delivered a presentation on how the Chief Data Officer (CDO) is fast becoming the next corporate rockstar. "*Rockstar?*" They questioned. Yes, total rockstar - except it's not just the CDO that fans of business value are flocking to, it's the data scientists and analysts that support them, playing to the tune of tapping data for insight to support more informed decisions and better business outcomes.

So it came as no surprise to hear about the fascinating story of Roskilde festival, who are using data and insight to better support their flock of rockstars and deliver the ultimate experience to thousands of music fans.

The story of Rio to Roskilde, as told by Per Ostergaard Jacobsen at Analytics Agenda in Sydney, the Co-director for the Centre of Business Data Analytics at Copenhagen Business School (CBS), started in back in 2012 in Rio at the Rio+20 sustainability summit which Per Ostergaard describes as "*lots of talking, but no action*". The team wanted to create a working model to test some of the great ideas generated from the event, and proposed the Roskilde festival as the perfect real-life experiment to test ideas and train sustainability models, bringing the knowledge and lessons learned back to Rio and to the world.

As the largest festival in Northern Europe, Roskilde very much reflects the workings of a city with 130,000 citizens, but for just eight days! With 175 acts and a community of citizens speaking the language of music, the 100% non-for-profit event consumes 200 tonnes of food and produces 300 tonnes of garbage - as such, the festival provides the perfect city lab to explore concepts around creating sustainable business and smarter cities.

The challenge: how can we build sustainable business models using big data to create mutual value for citizens and community, and for customers and business.

Challenge accepted, Per Ostergaard and his team looked to the data for insights - and there certainly was plenty of it! With the 15 data sources including over 91 million observations captured by the festival mobile app, 61 million observations captured on social media, 12,000 interviews, plus weather data and sales of tickets, merchandise, food and beverage - it was absolutely critical the team build a platform that could support both structured and unstructured data, captured in real-time, with the capacity to scale as data volumes increased. Per Ostergaard reflects the team was somewhat naïve when they started about the volume of data that would be generated during the course of the eight-day festival, but fortunately they made sound architectural decisions up front about the use of cloud computing and so could scale to accommodate as needed.

Common to big data best practice, the team created a landing zone where the data feeds were first fed for preliminary analysis. Of key importance was that only two people in the team had access to this landing zone, as the team took a strong stance on ensuring privacy and ethical standards in the use of customer data. As you can imagine, a wealth of customer data is captured during the event - not just the purchases they're making, but where they are located and moving throughout the event - so the critical first step was to depersonalise the data to remove any attributes that could be used to identify any one particular individual.

The data was then moved into a development zone for analysis, and later to a demonstration zone so key stakeholders could see the insights derived around the event.

Analysis of the event data uncovered key insights about how the food and beverage sales changed throughout the day, for example, strawberry smoothies were the recovery drink of choice by music fans and sales of roasted pork sandwiches peaked at 6pm, as well as the direct impact that weather had on purchases.

It also uncovered important associations across concert attendance that provides valuable insight when making decisions around community safety, customer service and location of merchandise stands, particularly around the movement of crowds both during- and after- each concert.

Understandably, the team expected festival attendees to go and listen to live music, but the data showed 10-15% of attendees never actually went to a concert! Instead, they attended the festival to socialise in the camp area and party with their friends.

One of the most fascinating perspectives Per Ostergaard shared was the concept of tribal movements - when people go to a concert they don't move as one person, they move with their tribe, or group of friends. When it comes to marketing, you have to make decisions on how to attract and serve the tribe, not the individual.

www.katsinsight.com

These are just a few of the insights uncovered by Per Ostergaard and his team that will be used by the festival organisers to plan and execute an even better event in the years following. The Rio to Roskilde story is a great example of how data can provide incredible insight into customer behaviour, to understand how to market and serve them better. But more than that, it creates opportunity to make smarter decisions around safety and environmental impact - lessons that can be taken from Rio to Roskilde, from Roskilde to the world.

Now, time to put together the business case for a site visit next year!

Why information about assets is your greatest asset

When a company's viability is determined largely by its investment in physical assets, information about the asset is an asset in itself.

Today, information is captured throughout the life of an asset and its individual components – it's how we use this information to make more informed decisions that can improve service levels and generate greater profits.

There are four key activities required to sweat an asset:

1. **Asset Management**

From the moment of purchase, key information about an asset must be stored to help manage and maintain the asset – such as make, model, warranty period, date of manufacture etc. Such asset management systems are a key source of information for reporting, and supporting important decisions throughout the life of the asset. It's also the system that can be used to track activities related to the asset – both usage as well as maintenance and investment.

2. **Asset Monitoring**

Throughout the life of the asset it's important to monitor both asset performance as well as the conditions in which it operates. This information, when available in (near) real-time, means we can be proactively notified when an asset steps outside of "normal" operating conditions and take pro-active measures to prevent failure, ultimately maximising the life of the asset and improving service levels.

For some industries, this also means being able to locate an asset! Whether it's a tractor, a plane, or expensive hospital equipment, knowing where the asset is located at any point in time gives us the ability to optimise its usage and evaluate where planned maintenance should be scheduled.

3. **Preventative Maintenance**

Waiting for an asset to fail can lead to catastrophic events, not to mention the financial impact of service downtime and industry-related penalties. Being able to identify key aspects to a specific asset's performance that identify those at high risk of failure gives the opportunity to conduct planned maintenance and prevent outages. It also gives us the insight needed to make an informed decision about whether to repair or replace the asset.

4. Resource Planning & Allocation

Not only must we manage the asset, but we must also manage the asset's assets — that is the limited financial and human resources available to maintain our most important investments.

Companies today are tapping into some of the technology available to support the above activities. For example, BMW Group are using predictive analytics and text mining software to analyse data on vehicles and repairs, vehicle error memories and dealer feedback, channelling insights back into BMW's working process to reduce error rates and save costs.

Power and Water Corporation, a major utility provider in Australia, consolidate and analyse maintenance and capital works planning. Together with Maximo asset management, they are able to effectively manage and plan the use of assets to meet the future needs of the growing Northern Territory population.

When investing millions (sometimes billions) of dollars in company assets, how much would you pay to add another 5/10/20 years to its life?

Before You Start

"Get your facts first,
then you can distort them later."
Mark Twain

www.katsinsight.com

Getting started on your data and analytics journey can be daunting, but it need not be.

The following are some of the best practice and learnings I've collected throughout the last 15 years working with clients around the world – including key trends in the data industry, demystifying buzz words like "big data" and "cognitive", and tips for driving success and ultimately business value from your investment in technology.

Generation D: Data-rich and analytically driven

There is a new generational gap emerging in the world of business, driven by a group of organisations we fondly refer to as "Generation D" — for data, which sits at the very heart of how these organisations think and act.

The bad news is, according to the statistics, chances are you're not working for one of them. The good news is, unlike many generational trends this is not related to age, so there is hope yet.

We know that data and analytics has the potential to impact how we work each and every day, and is already being used to transform entire industries for the better. Generation D organisations are data-rich, analytically driven, and setting new benchmarks in business performance.

Of more than 1,000 organisations that were interviewed, 7 out of 10 said they have more than enough data to get better insight into their business. And yet, only 1 in 5 organisations today use predictive and prescriptive analytics to make use of that data and support better decisions, more often.

Gen-D use analytical insight, cloud computing, and systems of engagement very differently to their counterparts. They are three times more likely to excel at knowing their customers and marketplace, two times more likely to automate process and decisions based on insight, and two times more likely to engage customers via digital channels such as social media and mobile devices.

And the effort is really paying off. Gen-D have an impressive scorecard in comparison to their peers:

- Share of wallet: +10 pp

- Customer retention: +6 pp

- Promoter/advertising scoring: +17 pp

- Rate of new product and service development released to market: +13 pp

- Employee retention: +6 pp

- Revenue through digital channels: +13 pp

Gen-D are also four times more likely to find new revenue streams, three times more likely to create new markets, and three times more

"Generation D organisations are data-rich, analytically driven, and setting new benchmarks in business performance."

likely to achieve operational efficiency — strategies that are crucial to survive and thrive in the current world of business.

Which begs the question, if you're not working for a Gen-D organisation, isn't it time you did?

The Chief Data Officer (CDO): Tomorrow's corporate rockstar

I had the privilege of spending time with some of Australia & New Zealand's Chief Data Officers (CDO) and up-and-coming data leaders – or as I like to refer to them, our corporate rockstars.

The CDO Forum provided the perfect environment for an open dialogue on how far the CDO role had come, and sharing expertise on how to successfully drive organisational change to make data a strategic asset across the business.

Some of the key insights from the opening panel discussion included:

- Adrian McKnight, CDO at Suncorp, touched on the importance of steering the role of the Chief Data Officer to one that is focused on the strategic use of data across the Enterprise, vs. an offensive role whose sole purpose is to protect against data risk.

- Kyle Evans, CDO at Corelogic, provided a unique perspective on the global trend that whilst the US has the highest number of Chief Data Officers, in is in fact the UK that has the highest number per capita – reflecting greater adoption.

- Dr Troy Delbridge, Chief Data & Information Officer at Private Healthcare Australia, shared a unique perspective on how much easier it is to get things executed when the CIO and CDO roles are combined – a trend we see growing particularly in small to medium sized businesses.

These insights were consistent with research into the role of the Chief Data Officer and what it takes to successfully deliver value from data.

There's no doubt data has become the next basis for competitive advantage. Take Pratt & Whitney for example – an organisation that some years ago launched the most fuel-efficient airplane engine on the market, providing them with a significant advantage over their competitors. As the number one cost to airlines today, any incremental benefit in fuel efficiency means significant impact to the bottom line and the ability to deliver a premium customer service. Two years after the engine took to the skies, Pratt & Whitney faced engineering and environmental tolerance problems, and with sensors generating terabytes of data every hour, they found it very difficult to know whether the tolerance alerts were a real problem with the engine or not. Given the significant cost to an airline when a plane needs to be taken out of the sky for maintenance, the engine's ability to deliver fuel efficiency was at risk of being overrun by the cost of unnecessary maintenance.

Pratt & Whitney turned to the data for the next level of competitive advantage. By analysing three years of engine sensor data, they were able to predict with 97% accuracy whether an engine was at risk of failure and dramatically reduce the need for unnecessary maintenance. Insight had become their competitive advantage.

Of course this is not unique to Pratt & Whitney.

With over 4.5 Quintillion bytes of new data being generated every day, there comes a significant challenge in how to capture, manage, maintain, secure, govern and derive insight from that data. But with challenge comes unprecedented opportunity, and the emergence of a new economy where insight is the currency and basis for value creation.

We spent time with innovative companies that had successfully derived business value from data to understand what they were doing differently. There were three key areas where Chief Data Officers from around the world had focused to drive effective change:

1. **Make data a priority.**

Chief Data Officers help the business make data a priority in order to leverage it as a strategic business asset. Collaboration and executive sponsorship is key to creating an enterprise-wide data strategy, where data initiatives are most successful when business stakeholders are included in the transition process and clearly understand the end benefit.

2. **Develop from within.**

Companies can dream of cutting-edge analytical capabilities, but those goals will remain imaginary without the personnel to execute their vision. To combat the shortage of available talent, Chief Data

Officers have started seeking and developing skillsets from within the organisation in order to execute their vision. They look for potential, not perfection.

3. Free the data.

Companies cannot unlock the full potential of their information if it is isolated in disparate locations. Chief Data Officers free the data and allow for the combination of data sources to uncover insights, encouraging business groups to share data and provide tools to give immediate, contextualised and integrated access.

And the payoff? Better business outcomes.

The biggest take away from the CDO Forum was that not all Chief Data Officers are created equal. The role comes in many different forms and flavours with one thing in common – a desire to translate data into tangible business value.

Big data? Big deal.

Ever heard the saying "It's not the size that counts, but what you do with it"?

No doubt you've heard the latest buzz words in the world of technology – the biggest of which is "big data". With exponential data growth, organisations are scrambling to understand how they will cope with the rapidly changing structured and unstructured data that supposedly now defines their business.

So what's the big deal with big data?

Essentially big data is defined by the 3 V's – **Volume, Velocity and Variety**.

Volume is the forefather of big data characteristics. A decade ago we defined large volumes of data in terms of Terabytes. Now, we talk Petabytes. And whilst technologies have existed in the market for years focused specifically on capturing, managing and understanding large volumes of data, it's important to note that big data is not just a big database.

Big data is also concerned with the frequency at which data is generated, captured and stored – that is, the Velocity. No longer are we content with loading historical data warehouses long after the trade has been executed or the fraudulent claim processed – there are growing business needs for real-time and near real-time processing of information.

The third V as it relates to big data is Variety. Data no longer fits into neatly structured tables, but instead incorporates geo-spatial, machine logs, sentiment, physical data points, social, text and web to name a few. Big data includes all data.

There is a wealth of articles and blogs written about big data on the Web if you need to know more. As you continue your research into this hot topic, just remember, it's not the size of the data that counts, but what you do with it.

www.katsinsight.com

Solving the issue of big data is no small feat. But even then, it's just data. As discussed in The Yin Yang of BI, capturing and managing data by itself does not deliver any value to the business. It's how you use and interrogate that data to derive new insight and make more informed decisions that can truly transform organisational performance.

So once you've considered the 3 V's of big data, consider the 3 W's of analytics – **Who, What and When**.

What business decisions need to be made? What insight can we derive from the information that we've captured to help support those business decisions? That is, we need to turn data into insight. Big data makes this process infinitely complex. For example, imagine capturing information about what people are saying about your brand in social media. In this case, a simple report would be near impossible to produce and likely to yield no real value to the business because of how much data it would contain. Using analytical methods that are designed to cope with the volume, velocity and variety of big data, we can derive insight into the sentiment and buzz words of the market as a whole – providing the business with insight that it can both understand and act upon.

Who could benefit from the information that we're capturing? Who needs to know what's really happening or what might happen in order to make better business decisions? To be of value, information, or more importantly insight, must be made easily available to the people that need it in order to support their business decisions. In today's pervasive world, that may be in the form of traditional reports and dashboards, or mobile notifications and disconnected analytical tools. In the sea of big data, there are countless amounts and types of information available – now more than ever it's important to ensure only what is most relevant to an individual decision maker is available as- and when- needed. This step in the process is how we turn insight into action.

When do they need to know in order to make a more informed decision? Information that comes in with greater velocity is processed in real-time for a reason – decisions need to be made in real-time. This makes it imperative to ensure insight is being derived at the time new information is captured and being incorporated into analytical decision management systems. Even when real-time is not a requirement, it is still an imperative to make sure the right information is made available to the decision maker in time to take action.

5 Big Data Resolutions for the New Year

Instead of making the same old resolutions this year to eat healthier, drink less alcohol and exercise more, why not make a change that will see drastic improvements to your personal and business success?

Here are my Top 5 New Year Resolutions to help you successfully tap into the wealth of data available to you to make better decisions, more often.

www.katsinsight.com

#1: I will focus on value

It's no secret that many big data projects fail to meet expectations, and in the vast majority of cases it's because the project never had a targeted business problem or defined outcome at the onset. Too often I see companies that want to leverage data in their business go to market for a "big data" tool, load all the data they can get their hands on into a mammoth mess, and expect magic to produce something of value. It simply doesn't work that way.

The most successful projects start with a defined business problem or opportunity, whether it's to increase the success rate of marketing campaigns, identify employees are risk of leaving, or improve the accuracy of business forecasts for example. Knowing the goal then drives the type and breadth of data that is required to derive a meaningful result, and that in turn influences the type of technology that can best support the data and analytical process, and ultimately produce a valuable business outcome.

No doubt many of you have well-formed thoughts about where you can get value from data in your business. For those that are still looking for inspiration and ideas, here's a few suggestions on how to get started:

- Read case studies about what organisations are achieving with data and analytics – peer organisations in your industry, your clients, your business partners, even organisations in other industries that might face similar business challenges to your own. ConAgra Mills famously looked to the aviation industry to find inspiration in how data can be used to optimise their business operations – sometimes finding a completely different perspective can spark a creative solution to your own challenges.

- Brainstorm ideas with subject matter experts from across your business and the industry. This means turning off technology, getting out pen and paper and/or a whiteboard with coloured markers, and getting the creative juices flowing. ASK: What aspects of your business need improving? What are your strategic growth areas? What critical business decisions are you and your teams making based on gut feel? How well do you know your customers?

- Once you have your list of business challenges/opportunities you want to address, conduct a Cost-Benefit analysis to help prioritise your initial focus. Grade each in terms of Time to Value, taking into consideration how easy/difficult it will be to get the specific data required to address that business challenge, and Value of Return to the business.

#2: I will not let a lack of perfection get in the way of progression

One of my biggest frustrations is watching a company spend years meticulously planning structured data models and integration points, only to finally produce a nugget of insight long after its value to the business has expired. Thou shalt not let a lack of perfection get in the way of progression. You don't need every data point cleansed, modelled and transformed to within an inch of its life in order to get started with big data analytics. It all comes down to the cost of inaccuracy. For example, if I said you could increase your marketing response rates by 20 points starting tomorrow, or you could improve it by 22 points but you had to wait 12 months to get started – which would you choose? Often the data we have today is good enough to get a substantial improvement on business performance. Unless of course your business objective is to reduce lives lost or another such critical business outcome where the cost of making a wrong decision is extremely high.

#3: I will bring in the experts

I've worked with various information and analytics technology over the past 15 years, and it would come as no shock to you when I say, what I knew 15 years ago, doesn't necessarily apply today. Whilst technology in general has been able to scale to meet the sizing demands of today's definition of "big data", it has not always been successful in adapting to efficiently deal with unstructured data found in social media, case notes, call logs etc., nor to deal with the speed at which data changes and needs to be analysed and served up to a decision maker. It's hard enough for those of us that work for leading IT vendors to keep up with the rate of change in the industry, it's even harder for those who have to do it on their own! Bring in the expertise you need to make your first project a success, and make sure the sharing of that knowledge is an integral part of the project so your teams can be self-sufficient with applying big data analytics to subsequent business challenges.

Resolution #3.5: I will not hire someone just because they call themselves a "Data Scientist"! I'm not usually a pessimist, but from experience, there are many who put "Data Scientist" in their title the minute it became a buzz word and started drawing the big pay checks. Do your research – hire someone who has a passion for data and analytics, and can work well with the business. (And when you find them, don't ever let them go!)

"I will <u>not</u> let a lack of perfection get in the way of progression."

#4: I will invest in a technology partner

There are some who still think the best way to invest in technology is to write a list of required features and functions, then peg vendor against vendor to find the individual products that together add up to 100% of the requirements list. How exactly does that help anyone achieve a business outcome? What you get is a list of ticks and a bunch of products that you or someone you pay has to make work, and no guarantees that when technology evolves (which it will inevitably do) it will still exist in the ecosystem.

Remember #1: I will focus on value!

I have an ongoing joke with my clients that if they don't want to invest in the technology, they can pay me a percentage of the increased revenue they get from implementing the analytics solution. Rumour has it a US organisation tried this once, and months later begged to renegotiate their contract after they realised how much cheaper it was to just pay for the technology solution and pocket the profits themselves!

Invest in a technology partner that makes your business success their priority – whether it's a Global technology company, Systems Integrator, or local IT services group – one that is committed to seeing you achieve real business value from your investment, and that will guide you through the evolution of technology so you continue to see value over time. Better yet, invest in a technology partner that is driving the evolution so you'll always be one step ahead of the game.

#5: I will review and repeat

Once you've achieved #1-4 and have successfully completed your first big data project, the most important step is to review what worked and what didn't work. Did you meet the stated business outcome? Did the technology partner you chose meet expectations? Does your team have the required skills to leverage big data analytics for the next business challenge? Develop a revised plan and move forward with addressing the next identified business challenge so you continue to get value from your initial investment.

The journey to Cognitive

One of my favourite poems growing up was "*If all the world were paper*", originally penned by John Mennes and James Smiths in 1658, because it made me THINK. It made me question the status quo. *What if the world was paper? What if the seas were ink?* What if indeed! For a child, the imagination ran wild. My grown up version takes on a slightly different perspective...

> If all the world were digital
> If all the tech in sync
> If all the data
> Were sliced and diced
> How could we outthink?

In a world where all businesses are digital and make data-driven decisions, how do you create and sustain a competitive advantage? Businesses today need to intrinsically understand, reason and learn - that is the foundation of cognitive.

With all the media and excitement around cognitive computing (including from me!) there has been a fundamental misconception about what cognitive really is. Here's the crux of it: Cognitive is not IBM Watson. But Watson is a great example of cognitive technology today!

IBM Watson was born out of a challenge to create a computer that could understand natural human language, investigate, reason and learn. Set the enormous task of beating the world's best Jeopardy champions, and like all transformative innovations, it failed miserably in its first attempts. But as the technology evolved, Watson learned the nuances of the human language - including how to understand questions and structure answers. The phrase "*the cat sat on the mat*" is not just a collection of words - they have meaning - and Watson understands the inference that the cat is on top of the mat. With the ability to read and understand, Watson then learned to investigate and to reason. With the world's information at its fingertips, Watson can trawl through unfathomable amounts of unstructured data - wiki pages, medical journals, clinical notes, maintenance records, legal documents - and make inferences about which information is most relevant to the question at hand, draw conclusions about what the answer is most likely to be, and recommend an answer based on confidence levels.

Most importantly, cognitive computers can learn. When a question is answered incorrectly, they incorporate that knowledge into its corpus to improve the ability to answer similar questions next time.

Cognitive technology has since been productionised and put to real work - helping clinicians diagnose and treat cancer patients, helping war veterans deal with life after the army, helping employees make critical decisions based on lifetimes of expertise, just to name a few. Make no mistake - cognitive will change the world. And yet I still get asked the question, what is the different between cognitive and a search engine like Google?

Here's the simplest way to describe cognitive computing:

Imagine you wanted to buy a car. Most likely you would first get on the Internet and search for cars. You'd collate information about dealers, models, styles, features, pricing, financing, formal reviews, social comments, and you'd work to read and understand in order to be able to make an informed decision about what is best for you. In the scenario of buying a car, the amount of information is consumable - but keep in mind, that is not the case in the world of healthcare or law!

Google does step one. I'm looking for an "*awesome raspberry red seven seater SUV*" - a Web search would return web pages that contained a high number of "*awesome*", "*raspberry*", "*red*", "*seven*", "*seater*" and "*SUV*" with no real understanding of what the words mean in context. Articles about an "*awesome blue five seater SUV*" would rank highly, even though it's not what I want.

Cognitive systems, on the other hand, mimic the entire human and information interaction, at epic scale. Cognitive can consume incredible volumes of information from web sites, manufacturer documents, maintenance records, and social media. It can understand that the colour of the car I want is not just red, but *raspberry* red. It understands the SUV needs to have seven seats. And it can return options to me based on whether people *like me* thought it was something like *awesome*. It doesn't just give me a recommendation, but also the evidence to support the decision so I can make an informed decision myself.

And when it gets it wrong, the next time someone asks for an *awesome raspberry red seven seater SUV*, it will provide a different recommendation based on what it learned from me.

That is the power of cognitive.

Of course, asking cognitive systems to help me buy a car is kind of like asking a doctor to put on a band aid! But you get my point.

What many people don't know, is that cognitive capabilities can be found across a range of technologies that have been given the ability to reason, act and learn.

Take for example the case for Next Best Action, which can be used to replicate and scale the human thought process of a highly experienced sales person in a cross-sell/up-sell situation. The solution will reason based on a set of business rules and patterns/trends that had been uncovered using predictive and advanced analytics, it will make a recommendation based on the optimal outcome of a cross-sell/up-sell, and if configured to, it will act - making an offer to a customer or recommendation to a call centre agent. Most importantly, it will make note of the outcome and learn from the result. If the customer didn't take up the offer - why? The outcome changes the prediction and action next time based on the ability to learn over time - just like an experienced sales person would.

Another example is the cognitive capabilities that have been built into modern Business Intelligence (BI) tools, designed to replicate and scale the ability of a human to analyse data. Imagine you had your own personal analyst - you'd give them data, they'd analyse it for you and make recommendations on insights they believe you'd be interested in. You would ask questions of them, they'd give you the answers, and they'd learn what you were interested in so next time they give you what you need in the first instance. Think of cognitive BI as like your own personal analyst. Just like a personal analyst, it will take your data and uncover insights it believes you are most interested in, presenting them in a way that best communicates that insight. You can ask business questions such as "*How did my sales track year on year?*" – cognitive BI tools understand natural language and translate it into a chart that answers your question. And it learns - as you interact (and don't interact) with certain insights, it better understands what you're interested in and uses that to serve you, and your colleagues, better next time.

The industry has many definitions for "cognitive computing", "artificial intelligence" and "machine learning" - and no doubt many would have differing views to mine. But fundamentally, we all agree we are entering an era where cognitive technologies are going to change the world of business.

A cognitive business is a business that thinks. That reasons and learns. It is an organisation that taps into all data - both structured and unstructured, both internal and external, both at-rest and in-flight. It is a company that uses technology to distil the 2.5 quintillion

> "A cognitive business is a business that thinks, reasons and learns."

bytes of data we create every day, down to a recommendation that a customer, an employee, a citizen can use to change their world.

A cognitive business can:

- Understand context and aspects of personality to personalise and deepen engagement with customers.

- Collate the most-advanced knowledge available and bring it to every employee to elevate the collective level of expertise.

- Interact with customers to create products and deliver services that continually learn and improve.

- Spot patterns in both traditional data sets and unstructured data to accelerate high-stakes research and time-to-market.

- Leverage vast quantities of both unstructured and structured data to continually improve its processes and decision-making.

So how do you get started on your journey to cognitive?

1. Design a cognitive strategy

Look at your products, services, processes and operations and determine which would benefit the most from the ability to reason and learn.

2. Extend cognitive with analytics

Understanding data is key. Make sure you can collect and curate the right data - structured and unstructured.

3. Move to a cognitive cloud

Make sure your business can get everything possible out of your cloud services, your data sets and your cognitive services.

4. Build a cognitive infrastructure

Businesses today need an IT infrastructure designed for cognitive workloads. They need to be able to handle the data and analytics required by cognitive services.

5. Adopt security for cognitive business

When everything is connected, everything is vulnerable. Make sure everything you do, every bit of data, every transaction is secure.

If all your world is digital. If all your tech were in sync. If all your data is sliced and diced. How will you outthink.....your challenges? Your competitors? Your limits?

Welcome to the era of cognitive business.

---

10 Reasons to get SaaS-y

Walking down the corridors at work I overheard the comment "*That girl's got SaaS!*" Hell yeah she does, and here's ten reasons why you should too.

www.katsinsight.com

When I joined the tech industry, solutions had to be built. Clients would invest capital expenditure on software licenses, the physical hardware required to run the software, the services to make it work, and the services to keep it working overtime. Not only was it an expensive way to invest in technology, but it required extensive research and an excruciating tender process because you had to be 100% confident that what you were investing in was going to work for your business.

Then came the era where consumer is king. The way in which we consume products and services in our personal life set the expectation for how we would consume technology in the world of Enterprise. Clients began asking: "*If I can rent a car, an office, a mobile phone - why can't I rent my software too? If I can simply turn on my tap when I need water, and turn it off when I don't, why can't I turn my computing power on and off when I need it too?*"

Hence the birth of SaaS - Software As A Service - where clients can simply pay a monthly charge for access to an application hosted on the Web. SalesforceCRM were one of the first pioneers to make SaaS a reality for Enterprise clients - when their Customer Relationship Management application was packaged up and offered "on tap" - clients simply paid a monthly charge for access to the application. Many other single-focused applications shortly followed, but the availability of complex analytical solutions took longer to be SaaS-ready.

Data is a highly sensitive asset, and it requires absolute confidentiality, and iron clad security. The last thing you want is someone else logging into your system and seeing all your customer data. Reading stories of high-profile security fails the likes of Sony and DropBox, you can easily understand the implication this has to your customers, and to an organisational brand.

In addition to the security elements, there is the complexity on the source of data streams - structured and unstructured, coupled with the need to analyse hidden trends and patterns, and be able to visualise and communicate insight to business users. You can't just secure the final report - you have to secure every byte of data as it is stored, managed and passed between various components of the solution.

The good news is with the rapid mainstream adoption of Cloud technology and increased security standards, what once were complex analytical solutions are now available using a simple SaaS model - covering everything from planning, budgeting and forecasting, to self-serve business insight and industry-specific analytical applications, through to complex big data platforms.

Customers getting SaaS-y today include:

- Mueller Inc, based in Texas, is a leading retailer and manufacturer of prefabricated steel buildings, roofing and construction products. To remain competitive, Mueller Inc must be as nimble as small companies and as scalable as larger competitors. It reduced time to value on processing new data by 90 percent, gaining insight at unprecedented speeds and uncovering answers to questions it had not yet considered asking, using an enhanced cognitive analytics platform. Mark Lack, Manager of Strategy Analytics and Business Intelligence at Mueller, describes *"using conventional BI often feels like hitting a golf ball down a fairway with a putter – it's a lengthy, multi-stage process. The cognitive analytics approach feels more like teeing off with a driver – it cuts out all those intermediate stages and gets you onto the green in one. I just load up my data and within 20 seconds, the solution presents me with visualisations of correlations that it has identified. This doesn't just mean that I skip many steps involved in conventional data analysis – I also get answers to questions that I hadn't even thought of."*

- FreshDirect is one of the leading online grocers in the US, fulfilling over 12 million orders since its inception. FreshDirect use software as a service to identify customer preferences across their digital channels and perform accurate customer segmentation in order to recommend the next best offer and encourage repeat business.

- Hothead Games is an award winning, independent games development studio, famous for creating games such as Scarface, Sea Stars, Zombie Ace and the Big Win Sports series. Hothead Games tapped into the SaaS to ensure the best experience for their players with fault-tolerance and performance across peak demand being hosted and managed by the big data experts. *"Leaving the database administration and performance tuning details in Cloudant's hands has freed up our team to focus on what matters most: making a great experience for our users."* -- Joel DeYoung, Director of Technology, Hothead Games.

- The Mears Group, a provider of housing repairs, maintenance and services in the United Kingdom, uses analytics software as a service to gain better visibility and deeper insight into its data and enable users to create insight without needing support from the IT department. Mears Group were able to analyse its large volume of IT-driven data to predict where to provide its housing repair and maintenance services, faster and easier than using traditional methods.

When you are in the process of investigating your next investment in Enterprise software, consider these ten reasons you need to get SaaS-y:

1. SaaS is significantly more cost effective.

Not only does it drastically reduce the upfront investment required, but you save on implementation and ongoing support costs. In the world of SaaS, the vendor is responsible for configuring and managing the ongoing availability of the system - saving you implementation and maintenance costs of both the software and underlying hardware.

2. SaaS gets you up and running faster.

Significantly faster. In many instances, you simply sign up for an account and you are up and running within the hour - versus the 3-12 month period it may have taken in the past to build the solution yourself. That also means radically reducing time to value.

3. SaaS lowers your risk.

Because you aren't responsible for supporting the system - if the servers go down, or the software fails - it's the vendor's responsibility to get the system back up and running. And for most SaaS offerings

"Using conventional BI often feels like hitting a golf ball down a fairway with a putter ...

the cognitive analytics approach feels more like teeing off with a driver."

Mark Lack, Manager of Strategy Analytics and Business Intelligence, Mueller

www.katsinsight.com

- that means 24x7 uptime without the drama have having to design and build a highly available solution!

4. SaaS solutions require less skills within the organisation.

Without the need to install, configure and maintain the system - that means less technical expertise you need to develop internally. Your teams can focus on high value activities like finding nuggets of insight that will deliver real value to the business.

5. SaaS is OpEx, not CapEx!

You simply pay-as-you-go. For many clients that makes it a lot easier to get CFO approval to invest, and it spreads the cost out over the life of the technology.

6. SaaS shortens your evaluation cycle.

Many SaaS-ready solutions offer a try-before-you-buy or a freemium version - where you can evaluate whether the capabilities are going to meet the needs of your organisation. This perfectly lines up with the fail-fast mentality - why spend months evaluating theoretical capabilities when you can roll your sleeves up and test it for yourself?!?!?

7. SaaS gives you better performance.

Underlying infrastructure is fine tuned for maximum performance by a team of technical specialists that know the technology better than you ever could, because more often than not, they helped write it in the first place.

8. SaaS gives you flexibility.

At the end of the month when you need more processing power to close off the books, or run that specialised marketing campaign, the solution will seamlessly scale up to support the additional workload, and scale back down when it's complete - making resources available for other users when they need it most.

9. SaaS means you can start small and grow with your business.

Buy only what you need today, and increase the number of users or data volumes as your business grows over time - without having to migrate or scale the underlying infrastructure yourself.

10. SaaS gives you an escape clause.

Because you pay month-to-month, you have the option to switch it off if the organisation is no longer getting value from the solution. Now the reality is some solutions require you to commit for a minimum period, and you might have invested time and skills learning the technology, so there will always be some level of sunk costs. But it's significantly less than if you purchased and configured the entire solution yourself, only to find it doesn't meet your needs.

In reality, not all solutions are ready to be delivered using a SaaS model, and not all companies are ready to move to Cloud. Which is why we still see many hybrid-cloud strategies that leverage a mix of SaaS, cloud, hosted and on premise custom solutions. At the end of the day you have to choose the right method of deployment that ensures successful delivery of the capabilities and business value - and you must always, ALWAYS, ensure SaaS offerings are underpinned by the level of security and governance you demand of all your Enterprise software.

Finally, make sure you do your due diligence on the vendor providing the solution. SaaS means you are putting your business in their hands - they are responsible for keeping the platform running that your business relies on to operate. You are trusting them with one of your most valuable assets - your data. Make sure they have the credibility that goes with that level of responsibility!

After all, they say data is the new oil. I wouldn't be handing over my oil reserves to just anyone.

Business Analytics: Design Outcomes, Not Solutions

The title Solution Architect is one I carried proudly for many years. After listening to Timothy Prestero's inspiring TED presentation *"Design for people, not awards"*, I'm thinking of changing it to Outcome Architect. I don't design solutions, I design outcomes. And here's why.

The world of technology used to exist to solve business problems. We'd evaluate the systems and processes that were "broken" and design solutions to alleviate the "business pain".

In his TED presentation, Timothy Prestero highlights the drawback of designing a solution to a problem, in that we might miss key factors that are important in determining whether the solution is used, and therefore, successful. A solution inherently focuses on the problem when what we really want is an outcome.

The conversations I have with customers today are not always about what's broken. It's about what's possible. Organisations are still concerned with fixing or improving key deficiencies in their business, but on the whole they are technically mature enough to know how to fix them (or at least where to start).

Organisations are now interested in understanding how technology can identify new opportunities for growth and competitive edge. This may come in the form of identifying new markets, more profitable products, more profitable customers and more efficient use of resources – all of which can generate outcomes of significant impact.

Take for example XO Communications, who sought to better understand their customers to protect existing revenues by reducing customer churn, increasing profitability and improving client service.

>The Outcome:
>
>26% increased customer retention
>376% annual return on investment
>Payback in 5 months
>Annual net benefit of over $3.8 million

Similarly, Cincinnati Zoo set a goal of increasing attendance and revenues by enhancing the customer experience for each visitor.

> The Outcome:
>
> 4.2% increase in ticket sales
> 25% increase in food revenues
> Payback in 3 months
> Total benefit of $2.2 million

First Tennessee Bank set the goal to better analyse the large volumes of customer-related data they had accumulated and derive insight of value to the business.

> The Outcome:
>
> ROI 642%
> Payback in 2 months
> Average annual benefit of $899,095

Whilst the numbers seem too good to be true, these types of outcomes are fast becoming the norm for business analytics solutions. This is partly due to the low total cost of ownership of analytics tools that are designed to balance business self-service with IT manageability, but also because I recognise that every business is unique and a cookie-cutter approach fundamentally will not deliver competitive advantage. My approach is to leverage the tools and technologies within the business analytics portfolio to deliver insight with significant business value – and that value is defined differently by each and every customer.

When it comes to deriving value from information, be sure to design for business outcomes, not technology solutions.

The Yin Yang of BI

If my customers were to describe me using a single word it would be: "*passionate*". And there is nothing that brings out the fire more so than hearing comments like: "*It doesn't matter what BI tool we choose, just get the data right.*" or "*The data warehouse is taking too long to build, just give them access to what you have.*" The former is more common amongst IT and consultants, and the latter, a common view of business groups.

It was decades ago when I was first introduced to the importance of balancing quality information with useful visualisation, which is why I'm amazed companies today still work with unbalanced solutions. It's what I call the "Yin yang of BI". Contrary to popular belief, Yin yang are not opposing forces like good and evil, but complementary opposites that interact within a greater whole, as part of a dynamic system.

Let's talk about the Yin.

A strong foundation for information management is key to any Business Intelligence solution – the ability to collect and store information that is accurate, complete, consistent, and available when needed. In an ideal world, it would include a single, consolidated data model containing the complete set of organisational data. The reality is that it often comprises a set of data warehouses or data marts, each with a set of accurate, up-to-date views of a business group or subject domain.

The Yang.

Equally important to a successful BI solution is the ability to get information into the hands of decision makers at the time it is needed, in a form that is easy to understand and interpret. For example, providing a dancing dashboard to technical analysts is counter-productive because it doesn't provide them with the view of information they need. Similarly, providing a detailed table of text to Senior Executives may not be an effective way to communicate organisational performance.

So what happens when the Yin yang is unbalanced?

With minimal investment in Yin, the business will make ill-informed decisions and start to distrust corporate information. This often presents itself in the form of Excel Spreadsheets and manual manipulation of data.

With minimal investment in Yang, a company will end up with a great source of information that no one can access or make sense of, and delivers no business value. This is when I start hearing the phrase *"The data warehouse is where data goes to die!"*

Companies that balance the Yin yang are better able to drive business value from their investment in information, that is, by getting the right information, into the right hands, at the right time.

They are also more at peace with the universe and sleep better at night!

Tackling the Tender: The 5 questions you need to ask

EOI. RFP. RFQ. RFI. NIT. ITT. PQQ.

A tender known by any other name would sound just as painful. Hours, days, weeks, months are invested into the tender process by both customers and vendors alike, but do they ever achieve what they are designed for?

Tenders range from short and sweet capability statements, to a comprehensive list of detailed technical requirements – all of which often fail to ask the questions that really need to be asked. A tender will most often ask the right questions, but do they ever ask the real questions that will determine success?

Here's my top 5 questions to ask of every vendor (with or without the lengthy technical questionnaire):

1. **Do you understand my business?**

Find out whether the company you are looking to invest in understands the industry in which you operate, the conditions you face, and the key drivers for your executive team.

2. Do you understand what I'm trying to achieve?

Find out whether they have really listened to you as you've described your key business pains, and whether they understand the goals you have set.

3. Do you understand what I need, not just what I want?

Technology is their expertise – if they truly understand your business they will be able to advise whether the technologies you are evaluating are right for the business problem you are trying to solve. They should also be able to demonstrate other areas of the business that can leverage the same technology and increase your return on investment.

4. Have you done this before?

Unless you like to live dangerously it's always good to know who their happy customers are. A logo on a PowerPoint slide is not enough – find out whether the solution solved a similar problem and if possible, talk to as many customers as you can to find out whether they are happy – not just with the technology, but the process and support they received from the vendor. User Group meetings are usually a free event and gives you access to a range of current customers.

If your project is truly innovative, it might be that no-one has done it before. That's okay! Find out what similar projects they've done and how involved the vendor was in the process – innovative projects are always more successful with a partnering approach.

www.katsinsight.com

5. Are you invested in my success?

Everyone will say *"Yes"* to this – it's often a gut feel question. Throughout the process, establish relationships that will stand the test of purchase. Better yet, get commitment from them to remain engaged throughout the project delivery. If you're in a position to offer a formal customer reference, that's one way to ensure they remain committed to your success.

Also, find out what their plans are for the future – you should never invest in technology that the vendor is not continuing to invest research and development dollars into themselves!

At the end of the day, a single feature or function will not determine whether a project is successful. Finding a vendor that understands you and is invested in your success will always lead to a more successful outcome for both parties.

A Word About Customers

When your feet hit the floor each morning your competitor should think "Oh crap, She's up!"

www.katsinsight.com

One of the most popular topics on **katsinsight.com** is anything related to customers – after all, this is the age of the empowered consumer. Data and analytics plays a critical role in understanding and better serving customers – here are a few of my most popular articles.

The Connected Consumer is King

Many talk about the interesting trends in economies driven by consumerism – with the rise of consumer spending on domestic products and services, fuelled by growing population and higher wage earners across many of world's growth markets.

Couple this with the rise of connected consumers – those living a digital lifestyle who expect to be able to run their lives through a smart phone and will quickly (and publicly) comment on the value of your brand when you fail to support them in doing so. Suddenly we find ourselves in an age where the connected consumer is king.

Today's consumers:

1. **Have increased spending power** – with more financial products and services offered on the market than ever before. From traditional financial institutions, to Telcos and even Postal organisations! This increases the importance of ensuring you have the right Credit and Risk Rating systems to approve the right customers and minimise the risk of financial catastrophe.

2. **Have access** to – *demand* access to – your products and services anytime, anywhere, on any device. With networks and devices growing in pervasive use and complexity, it is essential that you have smarter products and services to give your customers what they need, when the need it.

3. **Have a choice and aren't afraid to exercise it.** Consumers will just as quickly turn to social media for product advice than any well-trained sales representative, and expect a better buying experience when they are ready to purchase. Smarter commerce and analytics is essential in understanding what potential buyers want and need, to make sure you offer the right product or service at the right time, via the right medium.

4. **Demand goods in hand shortly after purchase**, making streamlined logistics an essential part of delivering the best buyer experience for return business.

5. **Are prepared to share** personal, confidential data with you, but expect you to have the right data governance and Security in place to protect their privacy.

There is no doubt today's consumers are connected to the world. The question is: Are you connected to the world's consumers?

"There is no doubt today's consumers are connected to the world.

The question is: Are you connected to the world's consumers?"

www.katsinsight.com

What Mobile & Analytics have in common: The Consumer

Ten years ago, when stuck in an airport lounge for an extended period of time, you probably would have read a book, a magazine, or opened your laptop to get some work done.

Nowadays, you're just as likely to attend conference calls, pay utility bills, conduct banking transactions, purchase clothes for the kids, and connect with family and friends through social media, all through the use of your smart phone.

A mobile device can be anything from a smart phone, to a tablet, to wearable technologies such as smart watches and fitness trackers. And they all have four characteristics in common:

1. **They are portable.** Where you go, they go – whether that's to the office, up in the sky, to the kids' swimming carnival, or sitting on the couch watching TV.

2. **They are always connected** – to the Internet, to Enterprise applications, to our family and friends.

3. **They are intelligent** – they can receive information, perform operations and share information.

4. **And they are personal** – most mobile devices are for a single user (unless of course you have young kids, in which case everything belongs to them!)

www.katsinsight.com

These characteristics make mobile devices the perfect medium in which to engage consumers, however many organisations today still view mobile as *just another channel* in which they can offer the same products and services they have today. For example, many banks see mobile as just another channel in which you can transact.

But let me cast your minds back to the time in which the Internet went mainstream. Similarly, many organisations saw the Internet as *just another channel* in which to offer their products and services. Companies like Borders saw the Internet as *just another channel* in which they can sell their paperbacks, and then the introduction of eBooks completely revolutionised the industry and sent them into financial distress. Companies like Blockbuster saw the Internet as *just another channel* in which they can rent DVDs, and then the introduction of streaming movies (both legal and illegal!) completely revolutionised the industry and sent Blockbuster into financial irrelevance.

So you have to ask yourself the question, is Mobile *just another channel*?

Fortunately, in IBM's 2015 survey of C-Suite Executives, 84% of CIOs rate mobility solutions as critical area for investment to get closer to customers. And 94% CMOs agree, ranking mobility apps as a critical part of their digital marketing plans.

The IBM Consumer Study (2015) surveyed over 110,000 consumers around the world, and showed a steady increase in our love of digital shopping – both online and Mobile. The percentage of consumers whose last purchase was made online was up from 15% to 18% in Australia, closer to 29% when we look at the global consumer base. No surprise that younger demographics (generations under the age of 40) were the biggest users of digital shopping – which means as our population ages, we can expect the proportion of digital shopping to steadily increase year on year.

Contrast that to the fact that 27% of Australians (and 43% globally) told us they had a preference for shopping online – and that presents a unique opportunity for organisations that offer a superior digital shopping experience to tap into a market that wants to shop online but haven't yet found the right retailers to serve their needs.

Now, let's say for arguments sake that you manage to get your customers to come in store. Guess what they bring with them? Their mobile device! When IBM asked consumers to rank who they would most trust to give them information and advice about products and services, retail employees and sales staff were ranked last on their list!

1. Friends/family

2. Product experts

3. Reviews on retailer websites

4. Reviews on independent sites

5. Manufacturers

6. Retail employee / sales staff

The second message heard loud and clear is that consumers want *"My Message, on My Terms"* – they want personalised interactions and offers, when and how they want to receive them. Given

Australia has such a high penetration of smartphones (78%) it makes them an ideal medium to engage and provide personalised offers and services. However, a generic message sent to a personal device is still perceived as spam – so there is a need to know your customers better so you can serve them better.

Many organisations I work with are still hesitant to ask for too much personal information from their consumers for fear of crossing that "creepy" boundary – so how do you know when personalisation becomes professional stalking? IBM asked consumers a series of questions to better understand what they were prepared to share with a trusted retailer, and 63% said they would happily share personal information in exchange for personalised offers. That includes 24% who will happily let you track their location, and 31% prepared to share their mobile phone number.

The most important think to consider, is that 50% Australian consumers (43% globally) want to be in control of this identification process. They want to be able to "opt in" for personalised services, and therefore, also have the option to "opt out" when the relationship is no longer serving their needs. This is compared to 24% who don't mind if organisations automatically recognise them by matching Enterprise data with social profiles. So for those of you that are still worried about whether collecting personal information about your customers will have a positive or negative impact on your brand – you simply need to ask them!

Given that by 2019, it is predicted that 49% of all online physical goods purchases will be made with a mobile device – now is absolutely the time to ensure you have a successful mobile strategy in place to capitalise on this growing market.

www.katsinsight.com

Of course a successful mobile strategy requires more than just an app, especially since 80% of all apps fall under the category of "throw away apps" – used once and then deleted. You may only get one chance to install an app on your customer's personal device – if you miss the mark, you miss the opportunity.

A successful mobile strategy requires:

- **A good understanding of your customer base** – not just their demographics, but their spending patterns, information about how and when they interact with your company, and their appetite to use mobile technology. Predictive customer intelligence requires behavioural data about what they purchase, descriptive data about who they are, interaction data about how they engage with your organisation, attitudinal data about what they think about your product and services, and the analytic tools that allow you to uncover the hidden trends and patterns that will give you insight into how your customers are likely to behave in the future.

- **A comprehensive analytics platform** that will allow you to not just understand the customer and know what offers they are likely to accept, but also know whether the rest of the organisation is able to deliver to expectation. Imagine running a successful targeted marketing campaign, only to have customers show up in store to find there are not enough products on the shelf to fill their orders. An Enterprise analytics platform supports all parts of the business – from Finance, to HR, to Sales, to Operations.

- **An agile mobile platform** to support the end-to-end delivery process for new and existing apps, making sure your mobile interface surfaces the right offers to the right people, engages them when and how they want to be engaged, and most importantly has the scalability and Enterprise-level security behind it to ensure you meet their expectations with privacy and responsiveness.

- **A customer engagement solution** to makes this type of personalisation possible at scale: across thousands of clients and millions of customers all using multiple devices and channels, with insight into how mobile interactions are working (or not working) so you can continue to adapt and innovate to meet their changing needs.

So what's the best way to start? First and foremost, you need to accept that it is a journey, and that you can't just flick a switch and go from generic to personalised mobile engagement in a single step.

1. You need to **identify the high-value opportunities** in your organisation – focus on the use cases that will get you a quick win.

2. **Establish the right architecture** that will meet the agile needs of the business, as well as the scalability and security requirements of IT. Plan for the future so that any technology investments made today can be used for additional use cases across the business.

3. **Prove value to business leaders** through pilot programs – measure the return on investment to grow confidence of the value that analytics and mobile can bring to the customer engagement.

4. **Scale by expanding** to additional use cases, and in doing so, transform to a data-drive culture.

Remember to leverage what you have – both in skills and technology, add what you need, move at your own pace (but always faster than your competition) and always, ALWAYS, act with governance and security in mind.

3 Caveats to Calling the Right Customer

The technology world is always abuzz with rumours of the latest and greatest Apple and Samsung smartphones. Which begs the question, with all this free publicity, are Telecommunication providers making the most of the opportunity to attract new customers and lock existing customers in to new contracts?

Many would say "*Yes*". Think again.

One thing Telcos and many retail organisations do well, is creating innovative and opportunistic marketing campaigns, tapping into existing trends and using the publicity to attract new customers. They're also very good at identifying customers coming up to end of contract and pro-actively persuading them to re-sign for another few years.

But are they calling the *right* customers?

In a world driven by increased revenue targets and counter-active cost cutting, it's not nearly as important to have the most customers than it is to have the most *profitable* customers. In a perfect world we could make attractive offers to every individual, but the reality is marketing budgets dictate a finite number of offers can be made. When it comes to knowing who to call, there are three caveats to consider:

1. What are they worth?

That's easy, right? Work out what they spent over the past contract period and assume that's what they'll spend in the next. *Wrong!*

Customer patterns change over time, even within the two years they may have been a customer. Imagine two customers who have spent the same amount on a mobile phone plan over the past two years. Except one of those customers spent more in the first six months when they were travelling internationally for work, and has since retired. Whilst the other had an increase in spending in the past six months as their travel for work increased. Which is likely to bring more revenue in the next contract period?

Fortunately, predictive analytics was designed to make the process of understanding the lifetime value of the customer a solvable problem, uncovering hidden trends and patterns in individual behaviours and extrapolating those into the future to understand their likely spend.

2. What will they pay?

Why offer a free phone to every renewing customer, when some of them would be more than happy to pay for (at least some of) it? The

"It's not nearly as important to have the most customers than it is to have the most _profitable_ customers" easiest way to execute a marketing campaign is with one offer for all. The smartest way to execute a marketing campaign is to tailor the offer to the individual customer and their willingness to pay.

Using predictive analytics and scenario modelling techniques, we can find an optimum price at which a particular customer will resign. And if we've already addressed Step 1, we know what the customer is worth and can model the combination of customer/product profitability.

3. Who will they tell?

It goes without saying we'd rather invest attractive offers in customers that will tell all their friends, and influence them to switch from other carriers, than one who will keep the benefits to themselves. This is perhaps the most difficult of the three to address, and is the newest member to the caveat list.

Social media analytics can help us to understand what our customers are saying about us in social media, and which of our customers are the most vocal and likely to become advocates for our brand. With the help of big data technology, we can trawl through petabytes of tweets, blogs and posts to understand sentiment and influence amongst our customer and their social networks.

Somewhat more specialised to the world of telecommunications, network analytics can help us to derive insight from call logs such as who our customers talk to and their circle of influence. Targeting those with influence over individuals who are currently signed with other carriers can give rise to indirect marketing possibilities that we may have otherwise missed.

With a wealth of information available both within the organisation and publicly accessible on websites and social media, there is no greater time in history to get to know your customer. Just remember to caveat before you call and ask yourself: What are they worth? What will they pay? Who will they tell?

You have 30 seconds to make the right decision. Your time starts...NOW!

A customer calls the help desk and gets routed through to you. They are not happy with the service they are getting from your company. You have to decide whether to make them an offer to keep them, or let them leave to a competitor. They may or may not be a profitable customer. They may or may not accept one particular offer over another. You may or may not have enough money left in the promotional campaign budget to make an offer. You have 30 seconds to determine the fate of this customer relationship and the impact on your revenue targets. Your time starts....NOW!

In this scenario, one call centre operator scrambles for their customer call centre application and executes a query to retrieve the customer's transaction history. They make an assumption that this customer will continue to spend the same amount in the future that they've spent in the past. They randomly select an offer that marketing has created for this month in the hope that this customer might be interested. They pray this offer hasn't been offered too many times already today. They make the offer, and leave it up to the Gods to decide whether this customer will stay with the company. The customer may or may not agree to the offer and continue their contract.

But what if this customer is not likely to be profitable in the future? What if this offer could have been given to a more profitable customer? What if they aren't interested, reject the offer, and out of frustration hang up and call the competitor?

A call centre operator, sitting in an office just around the corner from you, has the benefit of analytical decision management embedded in their call centre solution. When the customer calls, the system notifies them of the customer's history. More importantly, they are shown the estimated lifetime value of the customer. Using a combination of business rules, predictive models and optimisation techniques, the system makes a recommendation as to whether an offer should be made, and what offer is most likely to be accepted. The customer is overwhelmed with how well the company understands their needs, accepts the offer, and hangs up with a beaming smile on their face. The company prevents churn, retains high value customers, and increases revenue as a result.

So how does it work?

Analytical decision management combines known business rules, predictive models, and optimisation techniques to provide a recommendation on the best course of action. For example:

- **Business Rule**: Offers can only be made to customers over the age of 18.

- **Prediction**: The estimated lifetime value of this customer and the offer they are most likely to accept based on their demographic, purchase history and recent behaviours.

- **Optimisation**: Which offers should be made to which customers to maximise the revenue generated within our daily campaign budget.

By combining these different techniques, we are able to capture the experience and expertise of the organisation, coupled with the foresight of predictive analytics, and optimise the decision process to meet our desired outcomes – in this case retain high value customers and increase revenue within the constraints of the campaign budget.

You have 30 seconds to make the right decision, and the right decision is to invest in analytical decision management. Ok, so you have more than 30 seconds to make this important decision, but your time still starts…NOW!

Live The Dream

"Data is a precious thing and will last longer than the systems themselves."

Tim Berners-Lee

www.katsinsight.com

www.katsinsight.com

Of course data and analytics is not only used to increase profits, more and more it's being used globally to make the world a better place.

A big part of my journey over the past 15 years has been learning about how non-profit organisations are using analytics to fundamentally change lives – whether it be predicting and preventing crime in our streets, improving the successful training of guide dogs, supporting emergency crews in response to natural disasters, improving the success rate of children in schools, or finding more efficient ways to use our natural resources.

Their stories are also a great way to learn about innovation and doing more with less – as they more than anyone understand the need to deliver return on investment and maximise the use of scarce resources.

Here are a few of my favourite stories so far.

Big Data. Big Cats. Big Hearts.

As parents, you are constantly presented with opportunities to teach your children good (and bad) lessons in life. As it was for me, last month, when my two daughters wanted to explore their new found philanthropy, setting up a toy store at their local sporting club to raise money for World Wide Fund for Nature (WWF) so they could help save the animals.

Sitting there for four hours, encouraging them to be generous and sacrifice some of their much loved toys to protect our endangered species, it reminded me of one of my favourite examples of how data and insight is being used to fundamentally make the world a better place.

There are many things that threaten the existence of some of Earth's most incredible creatures, one of which is the illegal trade of endangered animals and their habitats.

The Environmental Investigation Agency (EIA) has for a long time been a leader in conducting covert investigations, using dangerous on-the-ground detective work to expose criminal organisations that thrive in local and global trade of endangered animals. A key influencer in the introduction of ivory bans, EIA are continuously trying to find ways to stay ahead of criminal gangs profiting from tigers, elephants and illegal timber. One mission close to my heart (and that of my budding global animal warriors) is their mission to protect the last of Asia's endangered big cats – including the tiger, leopard, snow leopard and clouded leopard – which face a multitude of threats from habitat degradation, prey and poaching.

It's no surprise that over the years, EIA have captured a wealth of information on the illegal animal trade – from video surveillance, to images, to documented persons of interest and their connections. However, because this information was stored in various formats and systems, and has grown significantly with more sophisticated criminal networks, it was difficult to manually map the various players and illegal transactions in order to find connections of interest and share intelligence with government and international law enforcement partners.

www.katsinsight.com

EIA turned to big data to find a better way to manage and analyse the wealth of information available to them, with the view to rapidly uncover hidden trends and patterns in time to take action. Using i2 software, EIA were able to map individuals to multiple aliases, merge and resolve common entities to streamline associations and present a clear picture of core involvement to aide suspect targeting. They were also able to critically visualise criminal networks to communicate with enforcement partners and execute a coordinated effort to identify and stop illegal trade.

Originally created to help Big Cats, the EIA Big Data platform has since been expanded to help with other illegal and destructive activities, including the rise in the ivory trade and the ransacking of precious forests. Together with big data, EIA are fighting crime with actionable intelligence so that my children, and yours, grow up in a world where animals of all species thrive in the wild.

Fighting Skin Cancer with Visual Analytics

With 50,000km of coastline, Australia has some of the most beautiful beaches in the world. Coupled with our love of sport and outdoor adventure, it comes as no surprise that Australia also has one of the highest incidences of skin cancer in the world – two to three times the rates in Canada, the US and the UK.

1 in 2 Australian men and 1 in 3 Australian women will be diagnosed with cancer by the age of 85, which brings not only a significant loss

of lives each year, but also costs the economy more than $3.8 billion in direct health system expense.

The sooner a skin cancer is identified and treated, the better chance of avoiding surgery and/or preventing death. Fortunately, humans are pretty good at identifying positive and negative cases of skin cancer, with the highest level of accuracy achieved at 84%. But imagine if we could increase the accuracy to more than 95%? Given Australian GPs are faced with over 1 million patient consultations each year for skin cancer, that could translate into 110,000 more accurate diagnoses each year.

You can see why I'm really excited about the project that IBM Research and Memorial Sloan Kettering Cancer Centre are currently working on – using visual analytics to increase the accuracy of skin cancer diagnosis.

Using cognitive visual capabilities being developed in the research labs, computers are consuming vast amounts of educational research data, and being trained to identify specific patterns in images and perform finely detailed measurements that would otherwise be too large and time consuming for a doctor to perform. This includes analysing the objective quantification of visual features – colour distributions, texture patterns, shape and edge information etc.

Algorithms are also used to measure the progression of lesions, such as aggressive growth over a short period of time, or deviations from what is considered "normal" for a specific patient or population.

This analysis will be provided to clinicians to highlight dermatological images that may signify disease.

In preliminary trials of over 3,000 cases of melanoma, atypical lesions and benign lesions, the technology developed recognised diseased states with 97% sensitivity, and is generating significant excitement about the future impact of such technology being widely adopted in the industry.

Once commercialised, the cognitive computing approach will be able to scan the images in less than a second, much more quickly than humans can, and provide insight to doctors so they can make more informed decisions about how to progress.

There is still much to be done. Memorial Sloan Kettering will continue to further refine and develop the process through larger data sets, but the initial results are extremely exciting and I can't wait to see this technology make it to Australian shores.

Race Across America with Analytics

I caught wind of a presentation being delivered at the Finance Forum in Melbourne, and was fascinated to hear how Doug Barton was going to make the link between Finance and cycling, or as he refers to it, *"what Doug Barton does on his day off"*.

I'll be the first to admit – I know nothing about cycling. I'm baffled why my father is happy to ride 100km with his crew just to "grab a coffee" and then ride back home. But add sensors, weather predictions and analytics – and now you've got my interest!

Race Across America is an annual transcontinental bicycle race from the west to east coast of the USA. Athletes from around the world race almost 5,000kms from coast-to-coast in what is recognised as one of the world's toughest endurance races. With entrants from over 35 countries, winning takes more than just preparation and luck – everyone is looking for an edge over their competitors.

Doug shared his personal story working with Dave Haase, one such ultra-cyclist. A five-time competitor in the Race Across America, Dave first rode the race back in 2004, and every year until 2008 where he reached his peak finishing in third place. This year, seven years since his last race, Dave decided to take on the challenge yet again, and pushing well into his 40s, turned to analytics to help him get his competitive edge over the rest of the field.

In theory, to win an endurance race of this nature you need to spend as much time on the bike and as little time sleeping as possible. In reality, it's not that simple. What's to say taking an extra 30-minute nap won't lead to better performance and faster speeds over the course of the day? You have your resources: your body, your fuel and your bike. You have your conditions. And you have your goal – to get to the end of the race as quickly as possible. So how do you optimise the use of your resources, within the constraints of the conditions, to complete the race as quickly as possible?

Dave and his team modelled his body, his bike and the race a lot like we model businesses.

They knew the velocity he needed to achieve on the bike is a factor of distance and time. They knew four turns of a 27" circumference wheel covers three yards on the road. They knew 80 revolutions per minute would drive him 240 yards. They knew the exact effort he had to exert and how far that would take him each day – and using sensors on the bike, how well he was tracking to those targets.

It wasn't just the bike that was instrumented to monitor performance, Dave swallowed a pill every 24 hours to collect vital data about how his body was performing, sending the results to his phone and the crew's iPad for analysis.

But it's not just enough to predict where Dave would be on the road at a point in time. They also had to use context and foresight to create their own luck. It doesn't matter what the weather is, you've just got to get up in the morning and ride against it, right? Wrong! We all know it's easier to ride uphill not downhill. But did you know that 60-70% energy expended riding a bike goes into pushing against the wind? As nice as it would be to have a tail wind from the Pacific to the Atlantic, a route over 5,000km changes direction, as does the wind.

Combining data from The Weather Company, they were able to predict his location more accurately, and the wind he'll experience at each point in the race. *"You can't choose the weather, but you can choose when to ride it."* With better insight, the team could see heavy winds ahead and predict whether it's better for Dave to slow his pace to avoid them. With seven stops across the eight-day race, the decision about when and where to rest can be critical to success. The team estimated smarter decisions about when to rest saved Dave 12 hours over the course of the race – that's 12 hours faster with no calories burned, zero watts required!

> "You can't choose the weather, but you can choose when to ride it."

Doug Barton, Director of Marketing, IBM

www.katsinsight.com

Of the 41 racers this year, only 18 finished due to heat exhaustion. Dave was one of them, not only finishing the race, but coming in second place – just eight hours behind the leader. In his fifth Race Across America, Dave Haase finished in an incredible 8 days, 20 hours and 6 minutes, with an average speed of 14.16mph. That's 2mph faster than his pace seven years ago when he finished in closer to 10 days. Dave's preparation and hard work paid off, with a little help from his crew.

Back to the original question – what does this have to do with Finance? Doug summed it up as this:

At the core of the Office of Finance, is comprehensive planning, modelling and monitoring how an organisation manages one of its most vital assets – money. Just like the world of ultra-cycling, it's critical that you have a good understanding of the resources at your disposal, the conditions you're working under (both internal and external), and the ultimate goal you are trying to achieve. This puts you in the perfect position to be able to leverage analytics to better predict what is likely to impact the bottom line, and optimise the use of your resources, under those conditions, to meet your corporate financial objectives.

Organisations today model their businesses with external data and advanced analytics, because they know:

- Weather is a leading indicator of future business trends such as retail demand or insurance loss;
- Social sentiment can be used to predict customer adoption or churn;

- Quota assignments can be improved with analytics used to model the potential across territories and sales rep types (hunter vs. farmer);

- Advanced analytics offers predictive insight into maintenance requirements eliminating down time and catastrophic losses;

- There is a direct link between economic activity and performance.

Next time you head out to take the wheels for a spin, spare a thought for how valuable it'd be to know what's coming next in your business so you could adapt and optimise the outcome. And take a moment to imagine what it's like sitting on that seat for 8 days, 20 hours and 6 minutes. *Yeowch!*

That's NEET! How Medway Youth Trust & SPSS are changing lives

Business analytics is not just about increasing revenue and decreasing profit, it's also about making the world a better place. I'm writing about the "business" of giving our most valuable resources a better start to life.

Medway Youth Trust are a charitable organisation based in Medway, UK, dedicated to helping the youth of today transition into their adult lives. With 6.2% of 16-19 years old in Medway not in education, employment or training (NEET), they face a high risk of unemployment throughout life and reliance on government assistance.

Medway Youth Trust invested in predictive analytics to address a number of concerns, primarily to help identify children at highest risk of becoming NEET in order to provide early intervention and change the course of their future. With a combination of demographic data, coupled with unstructured text in the form of notes taking during interviews, Medway Youth Trust were able to accurately predict what a youth would do after leaving school and focus resources on those most at risk of being unemployed.

Additional insight was found in the form of uncovering key factors that influence whether a youth will become a NEET. For example, if the youth was a teen parent it significantly influenced their unemployment risk. Similarly, female students whose surname changed in Year 10. These factors were taken into consideration when evaluating new programs and where to invest time and resources for greatest impact.

Without intervention, young people who are NEET are estimated to cost £13 billion cost in the form of government assistance, as well as opportunity costs of £22 billion by retirement age. These insights are not only helping to change the lives of the youths identified, but also the community as a whole.

Through advice and support for other youth charities, as well as incorporating insight from social media, Medway Youth Trust with the help of predictive insight are continuing to change the face of youth services and make a real difference in lives of children around the world.

www.katsinsight.com

"Children are the world's most valuable resource and its best hope for the future."

John Fitzgerald Kennedy

About the author

"Feed the family. Live the dream!"

www.katsinsight.com

www.katsinsight.com

About The Author

Katrina Read is a global Business Technologist and Technical Executive with expertise in customer success, data-driven marketing, mobile engagement, big data, analytics and cognitive business, and is passionate about using technology to make the world a better place. With over 15 years experience at the intersection of business and technology, she has inspired organisations across a range of industries to get to know their customers better by asking more questions, uncovering greater insight, and transforming their business with data.

Throughout her career, Katrina has been recognised for her achievements and leadership in the industry, including being awarded the Adacel Software Engineering Award, Worldwide Analytics Architect of the Year, Worldwide Solutions Consultant of the Year, **ARN Women in ICT Technical Award**, and **voted one of Australia's Top 20 Business Blogs**.

When she's not on stage presenting to audiences of over 1,000 attendees, or engaged in one-on-one discussions with clients about how technology can transform their business, she's capturing her thoughts on technology and innovation on **katsinsight.com**, or buying coffee for one of the many interns and employees she mentors.

Katrina is a renowned keynote speaker and has shared her passion on data and analytics with both business and technical audiences

www.katsinsight.com

around the world – from New York to London, Singapore and Sydney just to name a few. Her sessions have been described as high energy, intriguing, motivational and full of passion, with every session tailored to the audience for maximum impact and entertainment.

Katrina accepts a selective number of keynote speaking requests each year on topics such as:

- marketing in the era of cognitive;
- exceeding expectations of the digital and mobile consumer;
- thriving in a world of disruptive technology;
- the journey to cognitive business;
- transforming business with data and insight; and
- building a personal brand in the digital age.

For more information or bookings please connect via email: kat@katsinsight.com.

www.katsinsight.com

"Kat is what everyone has been looking for, a technical design guru who has a charming wit and drive that make it a pleasure to work with her."

BETH RUDDEN – DISTINGUISHED ENGINEER, IBM

"Katrina has a rare talent that straddles the divide between technologists and business allowing her to really understand the business value of technology. Her technical expertise is first rate and she can communicate intelligently to experts and generalists alike."

TIM YOUNG, VICE PRESIDENT OF MARKETING, WORKDAY

"Katrina is a transformation technical guru. Her unique ability to be able to understand not only the current and future technology landscape, but also how this relates to marketing, sales and other business functions makes Katrina an absolute business leader."

MICHELLE ZAMORA – HEAD OF MARKETING, IBM

"Combining her strong technical and solution understanding, solid business acumen, and great out of the box thinking, Katrina has a knack of easily communicating solutions to both technical, as well as, business audiences."

JOE KRISTO – CONSULTANT, TABLEAU SOFTWARE

"I first started working with Katrina when she was early in her career and she immediately distinguished herself as a rising star, creative, talented, with drive and a powerful ability to problem solve."

SIMON SPENCER – CEO, EDGELABS.IO

www.ingramcontent.com/pod-product-compliance
Lightning Source LLC
Chambersburg PA
CBHW070254190526
45169CB00001B/417